■ DRUGS
The Straight Facts

Designer Drugs

DRUGS The Straight Facts

■ DRUGS
The Straight Facts

Designer Drugs

M. Foster Olive

Consulting Editor

David J. Triggle

University Professor
School of Pharmacy and Pharmaceutical Sciences
State University of New York at Buffalo

CHELSEA HOUSE
P U B L I S H E R S
A Haights Cross Communications Company
Philadelphia

CHELSEA HOUSE PUBLISHERS

VP, New Product Development Sally Cheney
Director of Production Kim Shinners
Creative Manager Takeshi Takahashi
Manufacturing Manager Diann Grasse

Staff for DESIGNER DRUGS

Associate Editor Beth Reger
Production Editor Megan Emery
Assistant Photo Editor Noelle Nardone
Series & Cover Designer Terry Mallon
Layout 21st Century Publishing and Communications, Inc.

A Haights Cross Communications  Company

http://www.chelseahouse.com

First Printing

1 3 5 7 9 8 6 4 2

Library of Congress Cataloging-in-Publication Data applied for.

ISBN 0-7910-7638-5

YA
613.81
De

Table of Contents

The Use and Abuse of Drugs

The issues associated with drug use and abuse in contemporary society are vexing subjects, fraught with political agendas and ideals that often obscure essential information that teens need to know to have intelligent discussions about how to best deal with the problems associated with drug use and abuse. *Drugs: The Straight Facts* aims to provide this essential information through straightforward explanations of how an individual drug or group of drugs works in both therapeutic and non-therapeutic conditions; with historical information about the use and abuse of specific drugs; with discussion of drug policies in the United States; and with an ample list of further reading.

From the start, the series uses the word *"drug"* to describe psychoactive substances that are used for medicinal or non-medicinal purposes. Included in this broad category are substances that are legal or illegal. It is worth noting that humans have used many of these substances for hundreds, if not thousands of years. For example, traces of marijuana and cocaine have been found in Egyptian mummies; the use of peyote and Amanita fungi has long been a component of religious ceremonies worldwide; and alcohol production and consumption have been an integral part of many human cultures' social and religious ceremonies. One can speculate about why early human societies chose to use such drugs. Perhaps, anything that could provide relief from the harshness of life—anything that could make the poor conditions and fatigue associated with hard work easier to bear—was considered a welcome tonic. Life was likely to be, according to the seventeenth century English philosopher Thomas Hobbes, *"poor, nasty, brutish and short."* One can also speculate about modern human societies' continued use and abuse of drugs. Whatever the reasons, the consequences of sustained drug use are not insignificant—addiction, overdose, incarceration, and drug wars—and must be dealt with by an informed citizenry.

The problem that faces our society today is how to break

the connection between our demand for drugs and the willingness of largely outside countries to supply this highly profitable trade. This is the same problem we have faced since narcotics and cocaine were outlawed by the Harrison Narcotic Act of 1914, and we have yet to defeat it despite current expenditures of approximately $20 billion per year on "the war on drugs." The first step in meeting any challenge is always an intelligent and informed citizenry. The purpose of this series is to educate our readers so that they can make informed decisions about issues related to drugs and drug abuse.

SUGGESTED ADDITIONAL READING

David T. Courtwright, *Forces of Habit. Drugs and the Making of the Modern World.* Cambridge, Mass.: Harvard University Press, 2001. David Courtwright is Professor of History at the University of North Florida.

Richard Davenport-Hines, *The Pursuit of Oblivion. A Global History of Narcotics.* New York: Norton, 2002. The author is a professional historian and a member of the Royal Historical Society.

Aldous Huxley, *Brave New World.* New York: Harper & Row, 1932. Huxley's book, written in 1932, paints a picture of a cloned society devoted only to the pursuit of happiness.

David J. Triggle, Ph.D.
University Professor
School of Pharmacy and Pharmaceutical Sciences
State University of New York at Buffalo

1

Designer Drugs and the Brain

Designer drug (noun): "A synthetic version of a controlled substance (as heroin) that is produced with a slightly altered molecular structure to avoid having it classified as an illicit drug."

—**Merriam-Webster's Dictionary**

WHAT ARE DESIGNER DRUGS?

The term "designer drug" was coined in the mid- to late 1980s when doctors, scientists, and law enforcement agencies noted that, over the past few decades, the number of people who were attempting to illegally synthesize mind-altering drugs in underground "clandestine" laboratories was increasing dramatically. These "basement chemists" were taking the chemical structures of known legal drugs, such as the narcotic painkiller Demerol®, and altering them slightly (even by one or two atoms) to produce closely related *analogues* (molecules with very similar chemical structures). The idea behind this illegal synthesis was to create a "designer drug" that was hundreds or thousands of times more potent than the original legal drug. For a few hundred dollars in chemicals and lab supplies, drug makers and dealers could produce literally millions of dollars worth of illegal drugs. Also, since the chemical structure of the drug has been altered slightly, it was still perfectly legal.

The term "designer drugs" was originally used to describe the illegal analogues of the popular painkillers meperidine (Demerol) and fentanyl (Sublimaze®). However, in the 1980s, various analogues of the powerful stimulant amphetamine also started to emerge, most notably ecstasy and methamphetamine. Since these drugs were largely used by teenagers and young adults at dance clubs, parties, and all night raves, the term "designer drugs" often became replaced by "club drugs." Today, the terms "club drugs" and "designer drugs" are often used interchangeably.

The term "designer drugs" was a parody of the term "designer jeans," according to J. Morgan and colleagues in their discussion about Designer Drugs in the book *Substance Abuse—A Comprehensive Textbook*. During the 1970s and 1980s, Levi Strauss, Inc. was the leading manufacturer of denim blue jeans and was dominating the blue jean market. Hoping that consumers would pay little attention to the difference, other clothing designers started to produce "designer jeans" that were cheaper imitations, or copycats, of the original Levi brand.

Making designer drugs was legal for years, because at the time U.S. drug laws only prohibited synthesizing *exact* copies of approved drugs, while altering the chemical structure slightly and producing a closely related analogue was still perfectly legal. Thus, a basement drug laboratory could synthesize huge amounts of a designer drug without getting into trouble with the law. The same was true after the U.S. government banned the sale of AK-47 assault rifles, leading gunmakers to manufacture copycats with slight modifications so they were not technically AK-47s, but served the same purpose.

In 1970, the U.S. government passed the Control Substances Act, which classified all drugs into one of five categories, or "schedules." In effect, this law classified drugs according to how medically useful, safe, and addictive they are. The schedules are defined as follows:

Schedule I—The drug or other substance has (1) a high potential for abuse, (2) no currently accepted medical use in treatment in the United States, and (3) a lack of accepted safety for use of the drug or other substance under medical supervision. Examples: ecstasy, heroin, marijuana, and the hallucinogens peyote, mescaline, psilocybin, and LSD.

Schedule II—The drug or other substance has (1) a high potential for abuse, (2) a currently accepted medical use in treatment in the United States or a currently accepted medical use with severe restrictions, and (3) abuse of the drug or other substances may lead to severe psychological or physical dependence. Examples: cocaine, PCP, morphine, fentanyl and meperidine, codeine, amphetamine and methamphetamine, Ritalin®.

Schedule III—The drug or other substance has (1) a potential for abuse less than the drugs or other substances in Schedules I and II, (2) a currently accepted medical use in treatment in the United States, and (3) abuse of the drug or other substance may lead to moderate or low physical dependence or high psychological dependence. Examples: ketamine, anabolic steroids, some barbiturates.

Schedule IV—The drug or other substance has (1) a low potential for abuse relative to the drugs or other substances in Schedule III, (2) a currently accepted medical use in treatment in the United States, and (3) abuse of the drug or other substance may lead to limited physical dependence or psychological dependence relative to the drugs or other substances in Schedule III. Examples: Valium®, Xanax®, some barbiturates.

Schedule V—The drug or other substance has (1) a low potential for abuse relative to the drugs or other substances in Schedule IV, (2) a currently accepted medical use in treatment in the United States, and (3) abuse of the drug or other substance may lead to limited physical dependence or psychological dependence relative to the drugs or other substances in Schedule IV. Example: codeine cough syrup.

Schedule I drugs are the most highly restricted and tightly regulated, whereas Schedule V are the least restricted. Note that, in some circumstances, some drugs can be classified under more than one schedule. For example, although morphine is a Schedule II drug, it is considered Schedule III if it comes as a concentration of less than 2 milligrams per milliliter of water.

During the 1980s, it became evident that some "designer drugs" were more potent and dangerous than the original drugs they were designed to imitate, leading to many overdoses. Also, often times the drugs contained impurities that made them extremely toxic. Thus, in 1986, the United States government amended the Controlled Substances Act to include the Controlled Substances Analogues Enforcement Act. This law made it illegal to manufacture any drug that was "substantially similar" to the chemical structure of an already legal drug. Thus, simply replacing an atom or two in the chemical structure of a narcotic painkiller was no longer a legal way to create a drug that had similar effects to ones already made by pharmaceutical companies.

One thing is unique about designer/club drugs—they are all purely synthetic and made by chemical reactions in laboratories, often in garages or basements in residential neighborhoods. By contrast, other well-known illegal drugs come from natural sources such as plants. For example, cocaine is made from the coca plant, heroin is made from the opium poppy, marijuana comes from the cannabis plant, nicotine comes from tobacco leaves, etc. Thus, unlike illegal drugs that require significant interstate and international trafficking of the plant products (i.e., from South America, Europe, or the Middle East) before it gets to the user, the route from designer drug maker to designer drug user could be as short as a few city blocks.

DRUGS AND THE BRAIN

Designer drugs are mind-altering and can produce hallucinations. For these reasons, they are often called "psychoactive" or "psychedelic." Designer drugs produce their effects by altering the way nerve cells (*neurons*) in the brain communicate with each other (Figure 1.1).

Under normal circumstances, neurons carry electrical signals along wire-like nerve fibers called *axons*. At the end of each axon is a mushroom-shaped nerve ending called a *synaptic terminal*. When the electrical signal from the axon reaches the synaptic terminal, it causes chemical messengers (called *neurotransmitters*) to be released and secreted onto nearby neurons. This junction between a synaptic terminal and a nearby neuron is called a *synapse*. There are literally trillions of synapses in the brain, and each neuron can have as many as 100,000 different synapses on it. After neurotransmitters are released, they diffuse away from the synaptic terminal into the synapse and encounter proteins (called *receptors*) on the nearby neurons that are designed to recognize specific neurotransmitters (Figure 1.2). These receptors can cause the nearby nerve cell

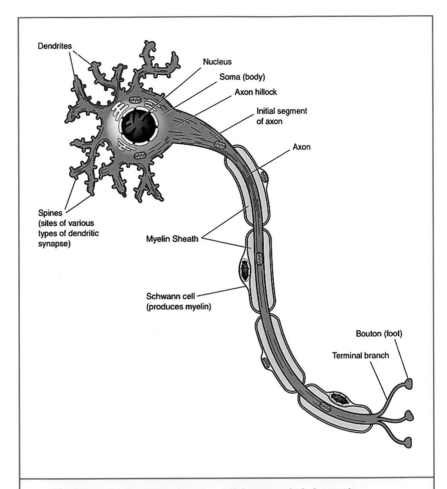

Figure 1.1 Neurons (nerve cells) transmit information throughout the brain and the body. A typical neuron is shown here. Electrical impulses are received by the dendrites and transmitted to the next neuron via the axon. The myelin sheath insulates the axon and increases the speed at which electrical impulses can travel.

to either become activated (i.e., passing along the electrical signal) or inhibited (i.e., do not pass along the signal).

Designer drugs, as well as other drugs like alcohol, cocaine, and heroin, produce their effects on the brain by altering the

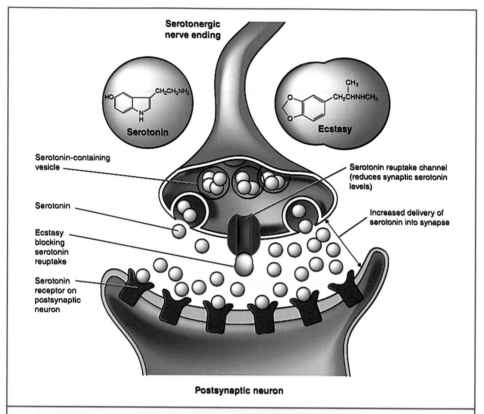

Figure 1.2 Serotonin is one of the brain's neurotransmitters. This image depicts serotonin transmission between neurons and the drug Ecstasy's effects on that transmission. Serotonin is normally removed from the synapse shortly after being released. Ecstasy blocks this mechanism, increasing the amount of serotonin in the synapse. This causes the postsynaptic neuron to be overstimulated by serotonin. Serotonin is one of many neurotransmitters that nerve cells can secrete. Other common neurotransmitters include dopamine, glutamate, gamma aminobutyric acid (GABA), noradrenaline, and endorphins.

actions of neurotransmitters and consequently how neurons communicate with each other. However, different drugs can alter the actions of neurotransmitters in different ways. Some drugs, like Ecstasy and methamphetamine, cause neurons to release excess neurotransmitters like dopamine and serotonin.

Other drugs, like GHB and Rohypnol®, can interact directly with the neurotransmitter receptors to either enhance or block the effects of the brain's own neurotransmitters. Still other drugs can alter the metabolic breakdown or clearance of certain neurotransmitters after they are released from the synaptic terminal, thereby altering how long the neurotransmitter affects the activity of other nearby neurons.

The brain has numerous regions that are each specialized for particular functions (See Table 1.1, Figure 1.3a, and Figure 1.3b). The effect a particular drug has on a person's thinking or behavior may depend on which region it is acting upon.

Table 1.1 Brain Regions and Functions

REGION	FUNCTION
Frontal cortex	Involved in planning, thinking, and decision-making
Motor cortex	Controls movement of the face, arms, and legs
Sensory cortex	Involved in perception of touch
Visual cortex	Processes sight and vision
Cerebellum	Controls motor coordination, balance
Brainstem	Controls basic bodily functions like chewing, swallowing, heart rate, and breathing
Hypothalamus	Controls metabolism, sleep, eating, and drinking
Limbic system*	Controls emotions, memory, and motivation

*Note: the limbic system is made up of several brain structures such as the hippocampus, amygdala, and basal forebrain (Figure 1.3b)

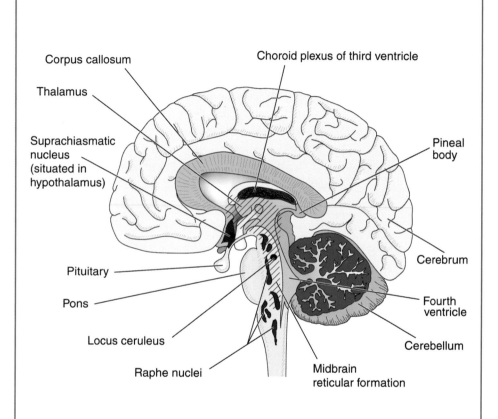

Figure 1.3a This diagram illustrates a cross section of the human brain showing some of the major structures. The brainstem, which governs functions such as breathing, heart rate, chewing, and swallowing, is made up of structures including pons, locus ceruleus, raphe nuclei, and midbrain reticular formation.

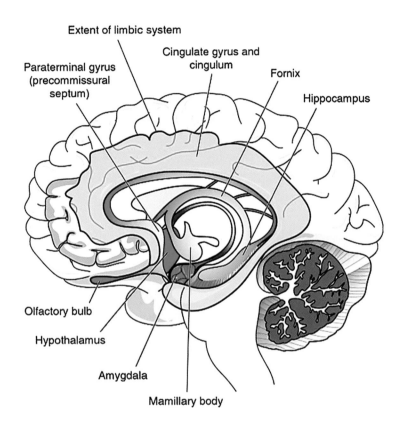

Extent of limbic system

Cingulate gyrus and cingulum

Paraterminal gyrus (precommissural septum)

Fornix

Hippocampus

Olfactory bulb

Hypothalamus

Amygdala

Mamillary body

Figure 1.3b This cross section of the human brain shows additional major structures. Note that the limbic system, which controls emotions, is made up of structures including the amygdala and hippocampus at the "core" of the brain.

2

Methamphetamine

COMMON STREET NAMES

Meth, Crystal Meth, Speed, Ice, Fire, Glass, L.A. Glass, Quartz, Crank, Chalk, Tweak, Tina, Jib, Yaba, Crazy Medicine, Poor Man's Cocaine, Hitler's Drug, Devil's Drug, Blue Mollies, Go-Fast, Mexican Crack, Shabu, Sketch, Stove Top, West Coast, Yellow Bam.

HISTORY AND LEGAL STATUS

Methamphetamine is a potent stimulant that was first synthesized by a Japanese scientist in the early 1900s as an analogue of amphetamine for use as a nasal decongestant, antiasthma drug, and weight loss aid. However, it was not used commercially until the 1940s when it was manufactured and marketed as "Methedrine" by the pharmaceutical company Burroughs Wellcome.

During World War II, methamphetamine was given frequently to soldiers to help fight fatigue and hunger, and to increase physical endurance. However, by the time the war ended, many soldiers were addicted to the drug and wanted to continue using it. Methamphetamine addiction became especially prevalent in Japan, where after the war Japanese soldiers were given access to military supplies of the drug to feed the addiction they developed during the war.

In the 1950s, many college students, athletes, and long-haul truck drivers started to use methamphetamine because of its ability to give the user energy and keep the user awake for long periods of time. During the 1960s, recreational use of methamphetamine increased dramatically when injectable forms became available that produced a much stronger "rush" than previously obtainable. Addiction to methamphetamine continued to escalate.

In 1970, the U.S. government passed the original Controlled Substances Act, and under this law methamphetamine was classified as a Schedule II drug in its injectable form and a Schedule III in its noninjectable (i.e., pill) form. However, a year later, both forms of methamphetamine were reclassified as Schedule II drugs. Today, it is still sold under the name Desoxyn® for a few medical uses, such as for the treatment of attention deficit disorder (ADD) and narcolepsy.

Throughout the 1980s and 1990s, the supply of methamphetamine continued to increase to meet the demands of an ever-growing population of meth addicts. Methamphetamine-related overdoses and deaths also increased. To stem the rising tide of meth-related overdoses and deaths, Congress passed the Comprehensive Methamphetamine Control Act in 1996, which established more rigid controls of ingredients in methamphetamine (such as pseudoephedrine—see discussion that follows) and imposed stiffer penalties for manufacture, distribution, and possession of the drug.

WHAT METHAMPHETAMINE
LOOKS LIKE AND HOW IT IS TAKEN

Methamphetamine most often comes in the form of white or clear crystals, which give it its nickname "ice" or "glass." Methamphetamine crystals can also be brown in color. These crystals are most often smoked with a pipe or snorted (Figure 2.1) and can easily be dissolved in water and injected intravenously. Methamphetamine crystals are also taken rectally. Meth powder and crystals often contain contaminants and impurities (including lead) from the chemical synthesis process that are often toxic. Approximately 50 milligrams (mg) of methamphetamine will give the user a significant high, although the absolute content of meth in a given batch of powder or crystals varies, making it difficult to know the precise amount of the

Figure 2.1 Methamphetamine can come in a crystallized form and be snorted with a "pipe" (shown here). Methamphetamine in this form is known as "ice" or "glass." The drug is also found in pill or tablet form, but produces a less immediate high, given that the drug does not directly enter the bloodstream.

drug that is being taken. Methamphetamine crystals cost anywhere from $300 to $4,000 per ounce, depending on where they are being sold.

Methamphetamine can also come in the form of colored pills or tablets (Figure 2.2), which many users consider safer than raw powder because they are less likely to be laced with contaminants. However, pill and tablet forms of methamphetamine often do contain impurities. These forms often produce less of a "rush" (the immediate pleasurable feeling produced by a drug) compared to when the drug is injected or smoked. This is because the pills must be absorbed through the gastrointestinal tract prior to entering the bloodstream and subsequently the brain.

Most methamphetamine in the United States comes from

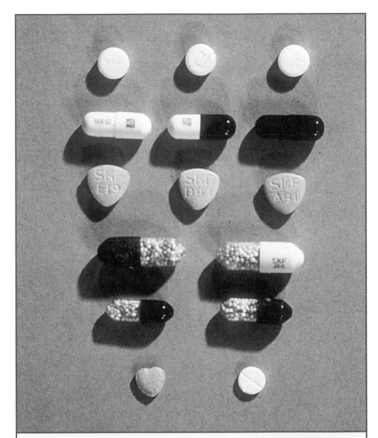

Figure 2.2 Methamphetamine can be found in pill form, as shown here. Many users incorrectly believe that pills are less likely to be laced with other drugs or contaminants.

underground "clandestine" laboratories in the western United States (primarily California) and Mexico. These labs are found in apartments, hotel rooms, basements, garages, rented storage spaces, and even moving vans. Lab operators often make their labs "mobile" so they can easily be packed up and transported. Meth labs are also often "booby trapped" with explosives to destroy the evidence in case they are discovered, and meth lab operators often arm themselves with guns and other weapons to defend their prized source of income.

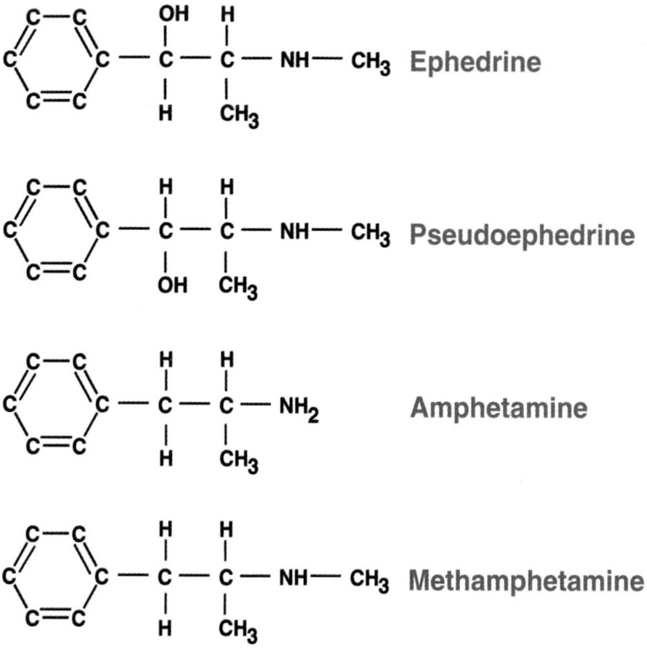

Figure 2.3 The chemical structures of the common cold and allergy medicines ephedrine and pseudoephedrine are very similar to, and can be used to synthesize, the illegal stimulants amphetamine and methamphetamine. Methamphetamine is much more potent than amphetamine.

Methamphetamine is synthesized, or "cooked," by a simple chemical reaction from its precursor pseudoephedrine (Figure 2.3), a stimulant commonly found in over-the-counter allergy and cold medications (such as Sudafed®). Because methamphetamine is made relatively easily from pseudo-ephedrine, many pharmacies and drug stores now restrict the amount of pseudoephedrine-containing medications that individual customers can buy to avoid the possibility of "stockpiling" pseudoephedrine for the purpose of making methamphetamine. Meth dealers and makers in the United

States have also been known to hijack shipments of pseudoephedrine-containing drugs en route to pharmacies in other countries, diverting them to the United States instead.

PSYCHOLOGICAL AND PHYSICAL EFFECTS OF METHAMPHETAMINE

When methamphetamine is smoked or injected intravenously, it produces a rapid intense "rush," "flash," or euphoria (very pleasurable sensations) within 3–5 minutes of taking the drug. This rush only lasts a few minutes and is not usually experienced after snorting the drug or taking it orally in pill form. After the rush wears off (usually after a few more minutes) the user becomes extremely alert, active, energetic, and restless,

Yaba—Methamphetamine from the Far East

Recently there has been a large influx into the United States of newer methamphetamine tablets from countries in the Far East, notably Thailand and Burma. These tablets are brightly colored, often stamped with letters like "WY" and are called by their Thai name "yaba." While the presence of the tablet is so new that use patterns are not yet known, the tablets are mostly found in Asian communities in California. The tablets are sent from traffickers in Southeast Asia to the United States by mail, overnight couriers, or on cargo ships. Because they come in convenient pill forms, many users take the drugs at dance clubs and raves. The colored pills look very similar to Ecstasy tablets (see Chapter 3). In addition to containing 25–30 milligrams of methamphetamine, yaba tablets also contain 45–65 milligrams of caffeine to give the user an extra energy boost. The pills may also be flavored to taste like candy. Some users even dissolve yaba pills in alcoholic drinks and coffee (so-called "bikers coffee").

and experiences very pleasurable feelings. These effects may take longer (15–20 minutes) to achieve if the drug is snorted or taken orally. Regardless of how it is taken, the effects of methamphetamine last anywhere from 6–24 hours (much longer than that of cocaine, which lasts 30–60 minutes).

When people start to use methamphetamine repeatedly, however, its psychological effects start to change. Repeated use causes tolerance to the psychological and physical effects of the drug—that is, the drug becomes less effective each time it is taken, causing the user to progressively need more and more of it to achieve the same desired high they have become accustomed to. However, some repeated users of methamphetamine may become increasingly sensitive (or "sensitized") to its effects. Repeated methamphetamine use can lead to "psychosis" (a lost sense of reality accompanied by hallucinations, delusions, and paranoia). A common delusion experienced by meth users is the belief that their skin is crawling with insects ("crank bugs"), so users may frequently pick at their skin, causing sores to form. Repeat users also commonly experience insomnia, mood swings, and personality disturbances, and because methamphetamine suppresses appetite, significant weight loss. Meth users may also become violent and aggressive, or engage in odd repetitive behaviors, such as being obsessed with dismantling and reassembling cars or other mechanical devices.

In addition to its effects on the brain, methamphetamine causes dramatic increases in heart rate and blood pressure. This is because methamphetamine causes increases in the secretion of dopamine, epinephrine, and norepinephrine in the heart and circulatory system, raising the user's heart rate to as much as 200 beats per minute (normal heart rate is around 70 beats per minute). Irregular heartbeats (arrhythmias) are also common. In addition, methamphetamine causes blood vessels to constrict, resulting in higher blood pressure in many parts of the body, including the brain. This "cerebral hypertension" eventually causes damage to the vessels, greatly increasing the risk for stroke or hemorrhage. Chronic methamphetamine use can also cause an inflammation of the lining of the heart.

Other effects caused by methamphetamine include headaches, decreased appetite, dry mouth, dilated pupils, trembling, chest pains, increased respiration and shortness of breath, hyperthermia (elevated body temperature), insomnia, and nausea and vomiting. In more severe cases (i.e., overdoses) it can produce seizures and convulsions, stroke, heart attacks, and death. The risk of encountering these more serious side effects are greatly increased when methamphetamine is used in combination with other drugs like cocaine, marijuana, alcohol, and heroin.

HOW METHAMPHETAMINE WORKS IN (AND DESTROYS) THE BRAIN

In the brain, methamphetamine causes massive amounts of the neurotransmitters dopamine, norepinephrine, and serotonin to be released from neurons in the brain, particularly in the limbic system and frontal cortex. Scientists believe the increased dopamine release in these brain regions is responsible for methamphetamine's ability to keep people awake, alert, energetic, active, and possibly addicted. Methamphetamine acts on a variety of brain regions to produce a number of different effects (Table 2.1).

Table 2.1 Methamphetamine's Effects on the Brain

EFFECT	BRAIN REGION(S)
Euphoria and pleasure	Limbic system
Decreased appetite, hyperthermia	Hypothalamus
Paranoia, hallucinations	Frontal cortex, visual cortex
Irritation, aggression, violence	Frontal cortex
Increased respiration	Brainstem

Prolonged release of large amounts of dopamine in the brain can be toxic to neurons, however, causing dopamine-releasing neurons to die. This damage may be permanent, as evidenced by brain scans on methamphetamine addicts which show that this damage is still present three years after ceasing to use the drug. Because dopamine-releasing neurons die off in regions of the limbic system, symptoms of impaired movement and muscle control can appear that are strikingly similar to Parkinson's disease (see Chapter 7). The death of dopamine neurons in the frontal cortex is believed to cause the paranoia and psychosis (hallucinations and delusions) seen in many chronic methamphetamine users.

STATISTICS AND PATTERNS OF METHAMPHETAMINE USE AND ABUSE

In the past, methamphetamine use and abuse in the United States was most prevalent in individuals who needed to remain awake and alert due to the nature of their occupations—long-haul truckers, for example—and in some "fringe" members of society. Today, however, it is predominantly used by white males in their 20s and 30s and is becoming more popular with teenagers at dance clubs and "raves." For these reasons, methamphetamine can be considered a "club drug." Methamphetamine use is also increasing amongst homeless people, prostitutes, and runaway youths.

Recent surveys indicate that as much as 4 percent of the United States population, including high school students, have tried methamphetamine at least once. Surveys of emergency room reports indicate that over the past decade, upwards of 3,000–4,000 methamphetamine-related deaths have occurred. There has also been a constant trend of over 10,000 ER "mentions" of methamphetamine since 1994 (Figure 2.4). In addition, thousands of meth labs have been raided and seized by law enforcement agencies in the United States in the past several years.

Historically, most methamphetamine use was concentrated in the western and southwestern United States. The drug is

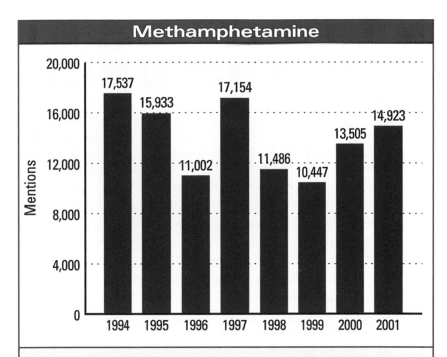

Figure 2.4 Although methamphetamine use has decreased slightly since 1994, the number of times "methamphetamine" is mentioned in emergency room patient reports in the United States is well into the tens of thousands, as can be seen in this graph. Many of these patients die from complications resulting from methamphetamine use.

still one of the most widely used illegal drugs in such cities as San Francisco, Los Angeles, San Diego, and Honolulu. However, increased methamphetamine use is starting to appear in Midwest states like Iowa and Nebraska, and even large cities on the East Coast such as New York City, indicating that its use is spreading across the entire country.

METHAMPHETAMINE ADDICTION
Methamphetamine is highly addictive, and people have reported becoming addicted to the drug after only taking it a few times. While some meth addicts take the drug once or twice a day, other addicts may go on meth "binges" or

"runs," taking the drug every 2–3 hours for several days without sleep. Heavy methamphetamine users tend to have poor hygiene and appear pale, and show a progressive decline in their ability to function in social and job-related

METHAMPHETAMINE AND ADOLF HITLER

Methamphetamine was widely used by soldiers in World War II because its potent stimulant effects kept them awake and alert for longer periods of time and increased their physical endurance. One infamous user of methamphetamine during wartime was one of the most evil men of the twentieth century—Adolf Hitler. Hitler started receiving daily injections of methamphetamine from his personal physician Dr. T. Morrell in 1942, and it was reported he could not function without his daily doses. Hitler also took many other drugs (perhaps over two dozen), including Cola-Dalmann tablets that contained caffeine. Hitler also dispensed methamphetamine to his troops so they could fight for days on end without sleep or food and outlast the endurance of enemy troops.

Hitler eventually developed hand tremors and problems controlling movement, which he would attempt to hide by covering one hand with the other, or by placing his hands in his pockets. These symptoms strongly resembled Parkinson's disease (see Chapter 7), which many scientists speculate may have been caused by brain degeneration brought about by Hitler's methamphetamine use. Other historians, however, speculate that Hitler's Parkinson's disease may have been caused by a virus or by the spirochete that causes syphilis.

Hitler's tremendous paranoia, lack of compassion and judgment, and violent and aggressive tendencies are often attributed to his repeated use of methamphetamine. These personality changes may have ultimately helped change the course of World War II and history itself.

situations. (This inability can persist for months or years after stopping use.)

One of the most devastating effects of methamphetamine addiction can be seen in pregnant women who are addicted. Exposure of a fetus to methamphetamine has been shown to cause limb malformations, abnormal reflexes, and behavioral problems in the newborn. Moreover, meth-addicted expectant mothers experience more premature deliveries and complications during delivery than do non-using expectant mothers.

Another consequence of methamphetamine addiction is increased risk for HIV infection and AIDS, since many meth users inject the drug intravenously and share needles. In fact, illegal drug use is one of the fastest-growing ways HIV is spread to other people.

Once a methamphetamine addict stops taking the drug, the withdrawal symptoms can be very severe and include depression and anxiety, increased appetite, fatigue, paranoia, irritability, aggressive behavior, and intense craving for the drug. Some of these symptoms can be eased with sedative drugs like Valium or antidepressants like Prozac®.

Although there are currently no pharmacological treatments for methamphetamine addiction, psychological treatments such as psychotherapy, cognitive-behavioral therapy (which involves changing one's thought patterns, expectancies, and behavior), and improving coping skills can be mildly effective in helping meth addicts stay clean.

3

Ecstasy

COMMON STREET NAMES

X, XTC, E, Adam, Eve, Clarity, Stacy, Love drug, Lover's Speed, Hug Drug, Versace, Essence, Decadence, Dex, M&M, Roll, Bean, Bens, B-Bombs, Disco Biscuit, Go, Morning Shot, Scooby Snacks, Sweeties, Wheels.

HISTORY AND LEGAL STATUS

Ecstasy, also known by its chemical name, 3,4-methylenedioxy-methamphetamine (MDMA), was first synthesized in 1912 by chemists at the Merck pharmaceutical company in Germany, who were searching for amphetamine analogues to use as new appetite suppressants. These chemists also synthesized a similar drug called 3,4-methylenedioxyamphetamine (MDA), which, as it turns out, is an active metabolite of MDMA. As MDMA and MDA are very closely related to amphetamine and methamphetamine (Figure 3.1), Ecstasy is considered one of the original "designer drugs."

Merck patented MDMA and MDA in 1914, but World Wars I and II sidetracked any further research on the drugs. Interest in the two drugs was revived in the 1950s by the U.S. military, but never went further than the animal testing stage.

Ecstasy remained largely unused as a recreational drug through the 1960s and early 1970s. However, in the late 1970s a biochemist at the University of California at Berkeley named Alexander Shuglin was approached by a student who claimed to have used MDMA to fix a stuttering problem. Shuglin decided to synthesize the drug and take it himself. He wrote a scientific

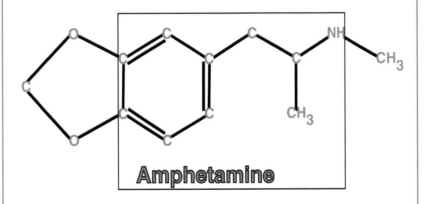

Figure 3.1 The chemical structure of Ecstasy (MDMA) is very similar to those of its cousins, amphetamine and methamphetamine. The structure of Ecstasy is shown here, with the structure of amphetamine enclosed in the box. Ecstasy contains an additional carbon ring and a methane (CH_3) group.

article that described the extremely pleasurable and controllable state of consciousness he obtained by taking the drug, and the mild, pleasurable hallucinations that accompanied these feelings. Based on his experience with the drug, Shuglin suggested that MDMA should be used by psychologists, psychiatrists, and counselors to help patients "open up" and explore their own feelings. A small underground group of psychotherapists followed his advice and used it successfully in their practices for several years.

But by the early 1980s, reports of Ecstasy's psychedelic effects leaked out to the public, and recreational Ecstasy use blossomed on college campuses in states such as California and Texas. This prompted the DEA to begin investigating the use, abuse, and trafficking of MDMA, which spawned media coverage and further public awareness of the drug. In 1986, the DEA indicated its intent to classify Ecstasy as a Schedule II controlled substance, citing that it still had potential for medical use in psychiatry. However, the director of the DEA, concerned about the potential for addiction to Ecstasy, deemed it necessary to classify it as a Schedule I controlled substance, the most restricted classification a drug can receive.

By the late 1980s, use of Ecstasy had spread across the United States and into England and the rest of Europe. Ironically, however, even though Ecstasy use likely originated in the United States, most (at least 80 percent) of the Ecstasy found in the United States is now produced in European countries like the Netherlands and Belgium. In 2001, U.S. Customs reported seizing over 7 million Ecstasy tablets that were illegally shipped to the United States. Penalties for Ecstasy manufacturing, trafficking, and possession currently include many years in prison and hundreds of thousands of dollars in fines.

WHAT ECSTASY LOOKS LIKE AND HOW IT IS TAKEN

Ecstasy most commonly comes in the form of a small pill (Figure 3.2). These pills come in a large variety of shapes and colors with various designs imprinted on them. A typical Ecstasy pill costs between $10 and $25 and contains 75–150 milligrams of MDMA. Since these pills look so much like candy, they are often concealed by mixing them into a bag of M&Ms® or Skittles®, or even placing the pills inside a Pez® dispenser. The pills are usually chewed or taken with a drink. In rarer instances, the pills are crushed into a powder and snorted or injected intravenously, or the pills are inserted into the rectum ("shafting").

Despite being in pill form, Ecstasy tablets often contain impurities that can be toxic and cause serious adverse reactions. Such impurities may include other amphetamine derivatives, ephedrine, and even heroin. Increasing reports of contaminated

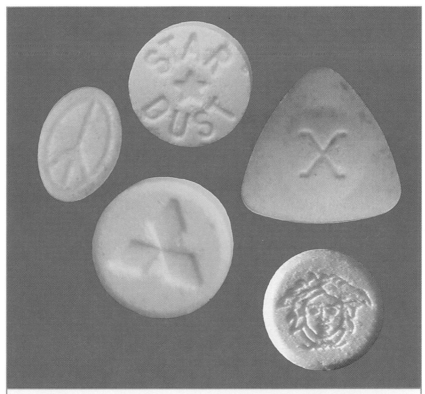

Figure 3.2 Ecstasy tablets come in many colors, with hundreds of different designs imprinted on them. The designs range from sports and car logos to catchy names, cartoon characters, and popular symbols, making them all the more appealing to teenagers.

batches of Ecstasy pills has prompted the need for "drug test kits," which test for such impurities, to be sold with the drug. Many rave parties now have booths set up where users can have their Ecstasy pills tested for contaminants.

PSYCHOLOGICAL AND PHYSICAL EFFECTS OF ECSTASY
Ecstasy has both stimulant and hallucinogenic properties. The effects of the drug begin approximately 20–60 minutes after taking it and usually last for 3–4 hours, but sometimes longer.

The most well-known effect of Ecstasy is its ability to produce intense feelings of happiness, well-being, confidence, loss of inhibitions, and closeness to others. Ecstasy also produces strong feelings of empathy (the ability to identify with and share other people's feelings) and often makes the users feel like they "love and want to hug everyone" (hence its name, the "hug" or "love" drug). Ecstasy can also produce a mild "rush" or euphoria, although not nearly as intense as

HERBAL ECSTASY— NOT REALLY ECSTASY

In recent years, a new drug called "Herbal Ecstasy" has been promoted as a natural and safer alternative to Ecstasy that may help with weight loss. Herbal Ecstasy supplements are sold in health food and drug stores, and marketed mainly to teenagers and young adults as being able to produce euphoria, increased energy, and heightened sexual sensations. They are also marketed as an aid in combating asthma. Common names for Herbal Ecstasy include Cloud 9, Rave Energy, X, Herbal X, Ultimate X-phoria, and Herbal Bliss.

Herbal Ecstasy is actually nothing more than a stimulant containing ephedrine and caffeine. The manufacturers claim the product is natural because the ephedrine it contains comes from the Chinese herb Ephedra (also called "ma huang") or other ephedrine extracts, and the caffeine it contains comes from the kola nut. Herbal Ecstasy can also contain other herbs such as ginseng, ginko biloba, green tea, and nutmeg. However, the FDA has warned that Herbal Ecstasy is just as dangerous as other synthetic ephedrine and caffeine products and can potentially result in irregular heartbeat, heart attack, stroke, psychosis, and death. These dangers are increased in patients with heart conditions, those who are taking antidepressants, or people who are overly sensitive to stimulants.

that felt after taking cocaine or methamphetamine. Other psychological effects of Ecstasy include increased excitement, laughter, relaxation, and talkativeness, and decreased feelings of anxiety, alienation, and aggression.

Because Ecstasy can produce mild hallucinations, it is often referred to as a psychedelic drug having effects similar to that of LSD. Unlike other psychedelic drugs, however, Ecstasy does not produce vivid perceptual and visual distortions, like walls and ceilings turning into liquid. Rather, the perception of colors, sound, music, and touch appears to be intensified by Ecstasy. In addition, the perception of time may be slowed or otherwise altered.

Despite the pleasurable effects Ecstasy produces in many individuals, some people report negative psychological effects while on the drug, including feelings of confusion, depression, anxiety, paranoia, and depersonalization. These problems can also occur when the person "comes down" from the high and the drug begins to wear off. Insomnia and irritability often occur as well.

In spite of the pleasurable effects that it brings about, Ecstasy is nevertheless a very dangerous drug. Ecstasy can produce sharp increases in body temperature (called malignant hyperthermia), which can lead to excess sweating, dehydration, and heat exhaustion, especially when the drug is taken at dances and clubs where room temperatures are abnormally high. Malignant hyperthermia is the most common cause of death associated with Ecstasy use. Another common cause of Ecstasy-related death is hyponatremia. Hyponatremia occurs when a person drinks too much fluid (in an attempt to avoid dehydration), which results in kidney failure, swelling of the brain, and coma. Ecstasy also increases heart rate and blood pressure, thereby increasing the risk of heart attack, stroke, or brain hemorrhage. Other common physical side effects of Ecstasy include dilated pupils, jaw clenching and grinding of the teeth (which is why many users chew on pacifiers), muscle tension, headaches, nausea and vomiting, tremors, anxiety, shortness of breath, faintness, chills, and blurred vision.

HOW ECSTASY WORKS IN (AND DESTROYS) THE BRAIN

Ecstasy produces its effects by causing massive amounts of serotonin and dopamine to be released from neurons in the brain. In addition, Ecstasy inhibits the ability of neurons to reabsorb these neurotransmitters after they are secreted. This has the overall effect of dramatically increasing the stimulation of serotonin receptors on nearby neurons. Ecstasy affects numerous brain regions, as described in Table 3.1:

Table 3.1 Ecstasy's Effect on the Brain

EFFECT	BRAIN REGION(S)
Euphoria, pleasure, empathy	Limbic system, frontal cortex
Hyperthermia, decreased appetite	Hypothalamus
Hallucinations, heightened perceptions	Frontal cortex, visual cortex, sensory cortex
Jaw-clenching	Brainstem

Ecstasy also stimulates the sympathetic nervous system (i.e., nerves located outstide the brain and spinal cord) causing increases in heart rate and blood pressure.

It is becoming increasingly evident that repeated use of Ecstasy actually damages the brain. Scientists believe that Ecstasy interferes with cellular and metabolic processes, specifically in serotonin-containing neurons, which eventually wither and die with repeated ecstasy use. This destruction of serotonin neurons in brain regions such as the limbic system and frontal cortex has been linked to depression, memory loss, and decreased cognitive ability.

ECSTASY AS A DATE RAPE DRUG

Ecstasy is not as commonly used as a date rape drug as GHB or Rohypnol, primarily because it does not incapacitate the victim or make him or her unable to ward off sexual advances. In addition, ecstasy is relatively insoluable in many liquids. Also, Ecstasy actually tends to make male users impotent and unable to achieve an erection. This impotence is increasingly common in men who repeatedly use Ecstasy. This has spurred the popularity of a new drug combination, Viagra® (a drug that helps men achieve erections) and Ecstasy, which male users take so they can remain sexually functional while high on Ecstasy. This combination is quite risky, however, with such numerous side effects as heart problems, high blood pressure, and even death, especially when taken with another drug called amyl nitrate ("poppers").

Nevertheless, there have been reports of Ecstasy powder being slipped into an unsuspecting person's drink. In such instances, a person under the influence of Ecstasy might experience confusion and impaired judgment, and may engage in behaviors that they would not normally engage in. Thus, Ecstasy is often still considered a date rape drug.

STATISTICS AND PATTERNS
OF ECSTASY USE AND ABUSE

As mentioned earlier, Ecstasy was given to patients by some psychotherapists in the 1980s to help them improve their communication skills and explore their own feelings. However, once the public became aware of Ecstasy's powerful psychological effects, illegal use increased dramatically, especially among high school and college students (Figure 3.3). In fact, recent polls and surveys indicate that between 7–11 percent of high school students have tried Ecstasy at least once, and this number is even higher among college students and young adults. As with other designer and club drugs, the majority of users tend to be Caucasian, although the drug is gaining popularity in African Americans, Hispanics, and other ethnic groups. Ecstasy users often tend to be from middle or upper class families, and thus Ecstasy is often referred to as a "yuppie" drug. Ecstasy use is vastly popular at dance clubs,

DRUGS AND ANIMAL RESEARCH

Research on animals has helped scientists to discover the toxic effects of Ecstasy on the brain. As in humans, when experimental animals like monkeys and rats are repeatedly given Ecstasy, nerve fibers containing the neurotransmitter serotonin start to die. Normally, the cerebral cortex (which includes the frontal, sensory, motor, and visual cortices) contains thousands of serotonin-releasing nerve fibers, which control mood and thinking abilities. In one scientific study, monkeys were given two 5 milligram doses of Ecstasy a day for four days, in an attempt to mimic an "Ecstasy binge" that human Ecstasy users often engage in. A separate set of "control" monkeys was given only saline. When the brain tissue of the monkeys was examined two weeks after giving them Ecstasy, many of the serotonin nerve fibers (depicted as pink in the photograph on the facing page) in the cerebral cortex had died or withered away. The scientists also examined the brains of a separate set of monkeys that had received the same Ecstasy treatment seven *years* beforehand and found that many of the serotonin nerve fibers in the cerebral cortex were still missing, although some had grown back. Scientists have recently found that Ecstasy also parties, and raves, and its use is on the rise at such venues as schools and shopping malls.

Ecstasy-related visits to hospital emergency rooms have skyrocketed in recent years, with approximately 250 reports of Ecstasy-related emergencies in 1994 to over 4,500 in 2000. The majority of the visits are Ecstasy-induced malignant hyperthermia, the risk of which is increased when Ecstasy is combined with other drugs such as LSD ("candy flipping"), psychedelic mushrooms ("hippie flipping"), methamphetamine ("up Ecstasy"), heroin ("down Ecstasy"), and cocaine, Rohypnol, cough syrup, and antidepressants.

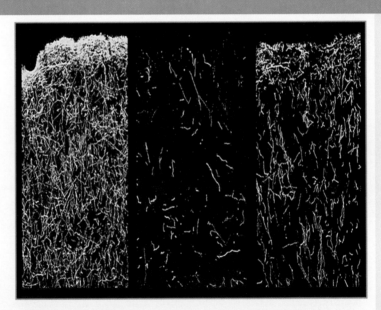

destroys nerve fibers in the brain that release dopamine, a neurotransmitter involved in motor control and motivation. It is thought that the ability of Ecstasy to destroy nerve fibers in the brain is linked to its ability to reduce memory capability and alter moods and motor function in human Ecstasy users.

Please see Publisher's note at the end of the chapter.

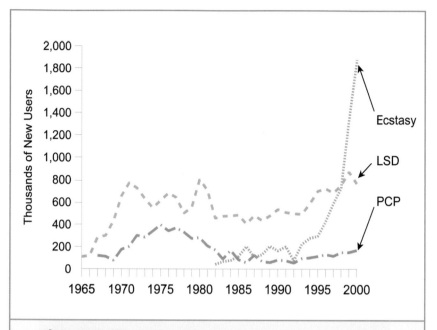

Figure 3.3 This graph shows the annual numbers of new users of Ecstasy, LSD, and PCP from 1965-2000. Starting in the 1990s, Ecstasy use increased in an extraordinary fashion and surpassed even the highest levels of LSD and PCP used. During this same timeframe, use of other hallucinogens stayed approximately the same.

ECSTASY ADDICTION

Ecstasy is mostly used as a recreational drug and is considered not as addictive as drugs like cocaine, methamphetamine, or heroin. However, there is growing evidence that Ecstasy can indeed become addictive if taken repeatedly. Repeat Ecstasy users often report that they develop tolerance to its effects and require higher doses to achieve the same high as previously experienced. In addition, some heavy Ecstasy users report intense cravings for the drug when they have not taken it for a few days. However, since Ecstasy is a relatively new drug and is often abused in combination with other drugs like heroin and alcohol, specific treatment programs for Ecstasy addiction are not well established.

RAVES

Ecstasy and other designer drugs are often taken at "raves," which are all-night dance parties held in warehouses or other large buildings. Raves feature loud dance music, lights, lasers, and other visual effects. Although they are often promoted as being alcohol and drug free, they are often a haven for illegal drug use. Raves came to the United States from Great Britain in the late 1980s and have become extremely popular in major metropolitan areas in the United States. Often sold at raves are overpriced water bottles and sports drinks (to combat the dehydration brought on by Ecstasy and other stimulants), pacifiers (to prevent teeth clenching by Ecstasy users), and glow sticks and menthol nasal sprays to enhance the effects of Ecstasy.

As mentioned earlier, Ecstasy can cause muscle stiffness and rigidity, so raves often have massage rooms. Many raves also have misting rooms with fans, where rave-goers can cool off from the hyperthermic effects of Ecstasy. Given that raves have these special rooms designed for Ecstasy users, it is not surprising that as many as 90 percent of all rave-goers have reported trying Ecstasy.

Publisher's Note:

Recently, one of the central studies showing evidence that Ecstasy can damage brain cells was retracted because methamphetamine, not Ecstasy, was mistakenly used in the studies' trial experiments. Nevertheless, there is still significant eveidence that shows the harmful effects of Ecstasy. These deleterious effects include damage to serotonin neurons, problems forming new memories, depression, and heat stroke. More studies must be conducted to provide irrefutable evidence about Ecstasy's specific effects on the brain, however.

4

GHB

COMMON STREET NAMES

G, Gamma-G, Georgia Home Boy, Grievous Bodily Harm, Salty Water, Scoop, Soap, Goop, Liquid X/Ecstasy (not to be confused with the real Ecstasy—see Chapter 3).

HISTORY AND LEGAL STATUS

GHB, short for its chemical name gamma hydroxybutyrate, is a potent sedative and a depressant of the central nervous system. GHB was first synthesized in the 1920s, although it was not specifically designed to mimic another existing drug. In the 1960s, GHB was developed for possible use as an anesthetic. However, the makers of GHB later withdrew it from consideration for approval by the U.S. FDA because of severe side effects reported by patients.

Despite these early warning signs of the potential dangers of GHB, several nutritional supplement companies started promoting GHB in the 1980s as a way for body builders to stimulate the production of growth hormones, enhance muscle mass, and reduce body fat. However, scientific studies have yet to prove that GHB can indeed increase muscle mass or assist in weight loss. GHB could easily be found in bulk quantities in many health food stores during this time and was also promoted as a way to ease anxiety and depression because of its potent sedative properties.

However, many reports of severe side effects and overdoses became evident, and in 1990 the FDA declared GHB to be unsafe for over-the-counter use and restricted its use to physician-supervised administration. Because of the FDA ban on GHB, street chemists and underground laboratories began to synthesize GHB illegally to fill the continued need for the drug. GHB use as an anesthetic still remains legal in many European countries, despite being banned in the United States.

By the mid-to-late 1990s GHB had made its way into the club, dance, and rave scene. Many adolescents found GHB gave them a pleasurable "high" and enhanced sexual experiences. However, reports of GHB overdoses and use as a date-rape drug, particularly when used in combination with alcohol, prompted the FDA in 1997 to reissue a warning against GHB use. Recipes and kits for making the drug began to appear on the Internet around this time.

In 2000, the FDA classified GHB as a Schedule I controlled substance. Punishment for possession, sale, or use of GHB became as severe as for other Schedule I drugs, including up to twenty years in prison. However, GHB was also subclassified as a Schedule III controlled substance, allowing for its medical use in patients with narcolepsy (see box on page 50).

WHAT GHB LOOKS LIKE AND HOW IT IS TAKEN

Raw GHB comes in the form of a fine white or light sandy-colored powder. This powder is rarely pure GHB—often the drug powder contains residues of the ingredients that are used to make it. These ingredients (GBL and BD—see discussion on page 47) are also commonly found in engine degreasers and floor strippers, and ingestion of these substances is extremely toxic to the human body. Thus, since the drug is made illegally in underground laboratories, there is no quality control, and any batch of GHB has the potential to contain one or more of these extremely toxic chemicals.

GHB powder easily dissolves in water or alcohol, and GHB is usually in this liquid form when it is distributed to the user. A standard "dose" of GHB costs anywhere from $5–$25. The liquid has a salty taste, much like baking soda, thus its nickname "salty water." The presence of chemicals other than GHB itself causes the taste to become very bitter and chemical-like. Some users tend to drink GHB by the capful, while others prefer to mix it into alcoholic beverages or other drinks to hide its salty taste. Since the liquid has no color or odor, it is easy to conceal in plastic water or sports drink bottles, or even mouthwash bottles or eye droppers.

PSYCHOLOGICAL AND PHYSICAL EFFECTS OF GHB

The effects of GHB usually start to take place 15–30 minutes following ingestion and can last for 3–6 hours. A typical dose of GHB can range from 1–5 grams. However, since the concentration of actual GHB in the mixture varies from batch to batch and vial to vial, it is extremely difficult for the user to know the precise dose he or she is taking. Thus, the difference between getting high and ending up in a coma can be only a few drops.

GHB has effects on the brain that are very similar to that of alcohol. In fact, many people take GHB to achieve its alcohol-like effects with less risk of a hangover. A low dose of GHB (less than a gram) causes the user to feel very similar to having 1–3 drinks—loss of inhibitions, feeling less anxious, and becoming more energetic, sociable, and talkative. Users may also experience mild muscle relaxation after a low dose of GHB.

A more moderate dose of GHB (1–2 grams) causes overall feelings of relaxation, well-being, and euphoria. Users also report an increased appreciation for music or dancing, as well as increased sexual drive and enhanced sexual experiences. Male users often report that GHB enhances their erectile capacity and intensifies orgasms. The user may also start to feel a slight loss of both balance and motor skills. Physiologically, this dose of GHB slows the user's heart rate and lowers his or her blood pressure and respiration.

Stronger doses of GHB (2 grams or more) start to produce signs of an overdose—e.g., slurred speech, severe motor impairment, and an overwhelming urge to sleep. In fact, the sleepiness produced by GHB can be so strong that it produces a coma-like state for which paramedics are needed to resuscitate the victim. Other effects of high doses of GHB include visual hallucinations, delusions, out-of-body experiences, vertigo (dizziness), disorientation, depression, and amnesia. Respiration is severely decreased at these higher doses, with reports of breathing rates as low as 6–10 breaths per minute. High doses of GHB can also cause one to lose control of their bladder or bowels. Other effects that are experienced at high doses include nausea and vomiting, seizures, respiratory arrest, coma, and even death, especially when GHB is mixed with other drugs like methamphetamine. All of these effects can have a quick onset, and unlike drinking alcoholic beverages, once the user starts to feel these effects, he or she is unable to "slow down" to avoid any further complications.

The effects of GHB are strongly enhanced, and much more dangerous, when it is used in combination with alcohol. Thus, the likelihood of the user experiencing one of GHB's more severe effects (i.e., seizure, coma, or death) are greatly increased when it is combined with alcohol. In fact, more than 80 percent of all GHB-related deaths involve the combined use of GHB and alcohol. GHB overdoses can also result from "boosting" (taking another dose before the effects of the first dose wear off). Since 1990, the Drug Enforcement Agency has documented over seventy deaths that were related to GHB overdoses.

As mentioned earlier, raw GHB powder is often mixed with other chemicals, including those found in engine degreasers and floor strippers. With repeated GHB use, these chemicals can erode the lining of the user's mouth and esophagus.

HOW GHB WORKS IN THE BRAIN

Surprisingly, GHB is naturally present in most cells of the human body at very low concentrations. Although the function of the body's own GHB is not clear, scientists believe it may be involved with cellular metabolism. GHB is also found in the brain and is believed to act as a neurotransmitter. It is believed that taking GHB drastically increases the messages carried by the brain's own GHB. GHB may also interact with a well-known chemical messenger in the brain called GABA (gamma amino butyric acid).

Table 4.1 lists the brain regions where GHB is believed to produce its effects.

Table 4.1 GHB's Effect on the Brain

EFFECT	BRAIN REGION(S)
Drowsiness and sleep	Frontal cortex, brainstem, hypothalamus
Euphoria, positive feelings, reduced inhibitions	Frontal cortex, limbic system
Hallucinations, increased sexual drive	Visual cortex, limbic system
Loss of balance, motor impairment	Cerebellum
Reduced respiration	Brainstem
Amnesia	Hippocampus (limbic system)

GHB may also act directly on muscles to produce relaxation and decreased heart rate.

GHB AS A DATE-RAPE DRUG

Although the most well-known date-rape drug is Rohypnol (see Chapter 5), the effects of GHB have also been exploited and used to commit sexual assault. In fact, the number of GHB-related sexual assaults in recent years have paralleled or even surpassed those involving Rohypnol. The number of GHB-related sexual assaults may be vastly underestimated because GHB is metabolized rapidly by the body and often not detectable in blood or urine when the victim reports the assault to the police. In addition, the victim is often not even aware that the drug was ingested.

GHB, GBL, and BD (GHB analogs) are used as date-rape drugs for the following reasons:

- They are colorless and odorless in liquid, and can easily be added to a person's drink without his or her knowledge. Although the drugs have a slightly salty taste, once blended with an alcoholic drink the taste becomes extremely difficult to detect.

- They have effects that are greatly enhanced when mixed with alcohol, making the victim vulnerable to sexual assault even after one drink.

- They increase sexual drive and reduce inhibitions.

- They cause impaired judgment and decision-making about sexual activity.

- They can cause the user to "pass out," making them unable to consent to or ward off sexual advances.

- They produce amnesia, so the victim may not even recall that a sexual assault has taken place and may not immediately go to the police.

GHB ANALOGUES

After GHB was banned by the FDA in 1990 for over-the-counter use, GHB chemists tried to circumvent the ban by developing closely related chemicals called gamma butyrolactone (GBL) and 1,4-butanediol (BD). The chemical structures of GHB, GBL, and BD are shown in Figure 4.1. When GBL or BD is ingested, it is rapidly converted by the body to form GHB, and the effects become identical to that of taking regular GHB. Due to the 1990 FDA ban, manufacturers of nutritional supplements previously selling GHB quickly reformulated their product so it contained GBL and/or BD instead of the

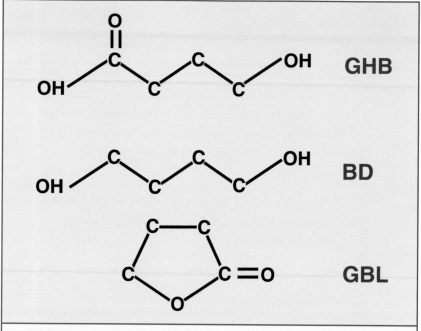

Figure 4.1 This diagram shows the chemical structure of GHB and its analogues BD and GBL. Notice the strong similarity between GHB and BD. Once ingested, both BD and GBL are rapidly converted to GHB by the body.

now illegal GHB. Such products were given names like Longevity, Renewtrient, Revitalize, and Blue Nitro. However, GBL and BD are no less dangerous than GHB itself. The FDA has issued warnings against the potential health hazards of and addiction to GBL and BD, and GBL is now considered a Schedule I controlled substance (BD is yet to be classified). GBL is an active ingredient in liquid paint strippers, polishes, and engine degreasers, while BD can also be found in various plastics, including floor coverings.

GHB OVERDOSES INSPIRE A FEDERAL LAW

Up until 2000, most laws regarding GHB and its analogues were primarily up to the legislature of each individual state. As a consequence, enforcement of laws regarding GHB was difficult. However, on February 18, 2000, President Bill Clinton signed a new federal bill into law regarding the use of GHB.

The bill, HR 2130, was inspired by the lobbying efforts of the families of two teenagers, Hillory J. Farias and Samantha Reid, who both overdosed on GHB in the late 1990s. The bill became known as the Hillory J. Farias and Samantha Reid Date-Rape Drug Prohibition Act of 2000. The law made GHB and GBL Schedule I controlled substances, which are the most restricted controlled substances under DEA jurisdiction. This classification now makes it a crime to possess, manufacture, or sell GHB or its analogues, with up to twenty years in prison for violating the law. The bill also mandates nationwide educational programs for students, teachers, nurses, sexual assault counselors, and emergency room staff on the dangers of date rape drugs (including GHB), symptoms of overdose, and penalties for their use.

Below are excerpts from the Websites devoted to the memory of Hillory J. Farias and Samantha Reid:

> **Hillory J. Farias.** 1978–1996. "Hillory J. Farias was 17 years old when someone slipped the deadly drug GHB into her soda. Also Hillory never drank, never participated in any drug use. She was very well respected by all of her classmates. She was going to be a senior in high school, she didn't attend her prom, never had a date. Hillory was cheated from having a happy and productive life. Hillory was the last person anyone would hurt. But it happened, and if it can happen to her, it could happen to you. Girls are not the only victims, men as well have been victimized, so please be careful. Remember a large percentage of victims know the person who drugged them." (*http://fariasfamily.homestead.com/Hillory.html*)

Samantha Reid. 1984–1999. "Samantha left for the movies on Jan. 16, 1999, with two of her girlfriends and two male friends from high school. GHB and/or GBL was slipped into her Mountain Dew® soft drink that night. Samantha was taken to the hospital with no vital signs and died after 18 hours on life support. The boys from high school are now serving 5 1/2 to 15 years in prison for the manslaughter death of Samantha." (*www.ghbkills.com*)

ARE THERE MEDICAL USES FOR GHB?

One of the ironic things about many abused drugs is that they often have a medicinal value and can actually be used to treat various diseases and disorders, given the proper medical supervision. However, the risks of abuse and overdose make them poor treatment options.

One peculiar effect of GHB is that it seems to reduce the symptoms of narcolepsy, a relatively rare sleep disorder. People with narcolepsy are excessively sleepy all the time and often have a condition called cataplexy, in which the person can suddenly and unexpectedly lose all muscle tone and fall immediately into rapid eye movement (REM) sleep (the stage of sleep during which dreaming occurs). Thus, a person with narcolepsy can immediately go from being awake right into REM sleep. (Normally, it takes at least sixty minutes to enter into REM after falling asleep.) These rapid transitions from waking to REM sleep can result in frightening hallucinations. Interestingly, bouts of cataplexy are usually brought on by laughter or strong emotional experiences.

In clinical studies, GHB has been shown to effectively reduce the symptoms of narcolepsy. These findings are quite

STATISTICS AND PATTERNS OF GHB USE AND ABUSE

GHB is currently extremely popular in the dance club and rave scene. It is also popular amongst the gay community as well as with exotic dancers and strippers. It is primarily used for its ability to produce euphoria, intoxication, and enhanced sexual feelings. Others still use it as a sleep aid or to enhance bodybuilding. Still others use it intentionally as a date-rape drug. Abusers of other drugs, such as cocaine or methamphetamine, often take GHB to reduce the withdrawal

ironic and paradoxical, given that GHB itself can cause excessive sleepiness and loss of muscle tone similar to that observed in narcoleptic patients. Scientists speculate that the sleep-inducing effects of GHB may counteract the abnormal sleep tendency seen in narcolepsy that contributes to the disease. This is similar to the paradoxical way in which the stimulant Ritalin is used to treat hyperactivity disorders in children. Scientists are currently investigating how the body's own GHB systems may contribute to the development of narcolepsy, and they are exploring possible GHB-like medications that can be used to treat the disorder without all the dangerous side effects. Because there are so few effective medications to treat narcolepsy, in July 2002 the FDA approved the use of GHB under the trade name Xyrem® for the treatment of the disease.

GHB has also been reported to have other medical benefits, such as a sleep aid for people suffering from temporary insomnia and for treating alcohol withdrawal and alcoholism. However, the risks and dangers of taking GHB, especially in combination with alcohol, have prohibited the FDA from approving its use for conditions other than narcolepsy.

symptoms that occur after the effects of these stimulants wear off.

Regardless of the purpose, GHB is primarily taken by teenagers and young adults ages 18–25. A recent survey found that in 2001, approximately 1 percent of eighth grade students had tried GHB in the past year, whereas 1.6 percent of high school seniors had tried the drug. On college campuses, the use of GHB is even more prevalent, with as many as 20 percent of all college students having tried GHB or knowing someone who has.

To determine the prevalence of GHB-related overdoses, the Drug Abuse Warning Network recently surveyed reports from emergency rooms across the United States for mentions of "GHB." As seen in Figure 4.2, the number of times GHB has been mentioned in emergency room visit reports has skyrocketed in the past decade, with around 55 in 1994 to over 4,000 in 2000. Of GHB-related emergencies, most victims appear to be middle class, male Caucasians. More than 75 percent of all GHB-related emergency room visits have also involved the use of alcohol, showing how dangerous the combination of the two drugs can be. GHB-related emergency room visits that involve the co-use of cocaine, Ecstasy, and marijuana occur less frequently than with alcohol.

GHB ADDICTION

Although GHB is primarily used for recreational purposes, cases of addiction to GHB have been reported. Some GHB users go on binges during which they take GHB around the clock (every 2–4 hours) for a few days. As the user takes additional doses, he or she develops tolerance to the effects of the drug (i.e., GHB becomes less effective with subsequent doses, so the user takes even more). Eventually, the binge GHB user exhibits signs of withdrawal, such as anxiety, insomnia, delirium and hallucinations, muscle cramping and tremors, and tachycardia (abnormally fast heart rate). GHB is

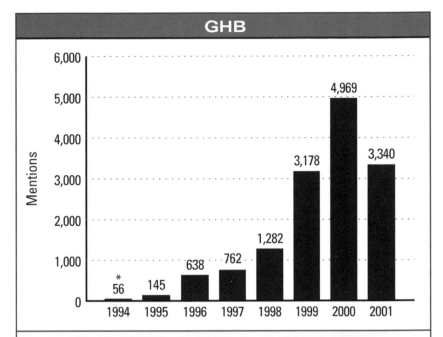

Figure 4.2 The number of emergency room cases resulting from GHB use has increased significantly since the early 1990s. As can be seen on this graph, the number of emergency room reports more than doubled in the course of two years (1998 and 2000). Although fewer cases were reported in 2001 than 2000, GHB use is still a problem.

* The estimate for this year was significantly different ($p < 0.05$) than the estimate for 2001.

eliminated rapidly from the body, so in the binge GHB user symptoms of withdrawal may begin within a few hours of the last dose. Despite being eliminated from the body quickly, the withdrawal symptoms may persist for weeks or months.

Because GHB use and abuse has only recently become prevalent, treatment programs designed specifically for the GHB addict have not yet been developed.

5

Rohypnol

COMMON STREET NAMES

Roofies, Rophies, Ruffies, Roche, Roach, Rope, Ropies, Rib, Circles, Mexican Valium, R-2, Date Rape Pill, Forget-Me Pill.

HISTORY AND LEGAL STATUS

Rohypnol is the trade name for flunitrazepam (pronounced "floo-nigh-trays-eh-pam"), a drug that belongs to a class of drugs called benzodiazepines (pronounced "ben-zoh-di-ayz-eh-peens"). Other well-known benzodiazepines include Valium and Xanax. Benzodiazepines are primarily prescribed by doctors to treat anxiety, panic attacks, and insomnia.

Rohypnol was first manufactured and patented by the pharmaceutical company Hoffman-La Roche in 1963 as a way to treat insomnia and anxiety. Rohypnol was intended to be an analogue of Valium and other benzodiazepine drugs. In 1984, Rohypnol became classified as a Schedule IV controlled substance in the DEA. However, due to increasing reports of Rohypnol abuse and misuse, it was reclassified as a Schedule III drug in 1995, requiring more thorough record keeping by manufacturers, pharmacies, and doctors. Further increases in illegal use of the drug in the United States during the late 1990s has prompted the DEA to consider classifying it as a Schedule I controlled substance throughout the United States, although to date only several states have actually done so. Despite heavy restrictions on its use in the United States, Rohypnol is still sold legally by prescription for the treatment of insomnia and as a sedative prior to surgery in many Latin American and European countries. Rohypnol is difficult to synthesize and is not made in underground "clandestine" laboratories.

In the 1990s, Rohypnol became known as the "date-rape drug" because of its ability to physically and mentally incapacitate the user, allowing sexual advances to proceed virtually unimpeded. Extensive use of Rohypnol in sexual assaults and "date rapes" led Congress to pass the Drug-Induced Rape Prevention and Punishment Act of 1996. This law increased prison time for persons convicted of using Rohypnol (or other controlled substances) to commit a violent crime such as rape. Importation and distribution of one or more grams of Rohypnol became punishable by up to twenty years in prison, whereas possession of smaller amounts of the drug became punishable by up to three years in prison and a fine.

WHAT ROHYPNOL LOOKS LIKE
AND HOW IT IS TAKEN

Rohypnol was originally manufactured in the form of a small round white pill, each a little over half a centimeter in diameter (see Figure 5.1), with the word "Roche" stamped on it. Each pill contained 1–2 milligrams of the drug. On the street, these pills cost anywhere from $2–$10 each. While many illicit users of Rohypnol chose to take the pill orally, some ground the pills into a fine white powder so it could be snorted or mixed into a drink.

In response to the alarming increases in reported date rapes that used Rohypnol to incapacitate the victim, Rohypnol manufacturer Hoffman-La Roche decided to change the shape and color of the pill in the late 1990s. Rohypnol was changed to a green oval tablet with the number "542" stamped on it. However, the manufacturers also added something else—a dye. According to Hoffman-La Roche, if the newer Rohypnol pills were crushed into a powder and slipped into someone's drink, the dye would turn the drink blue or green, alerting the potential victim that his or her drink had been tampered with (unless, of

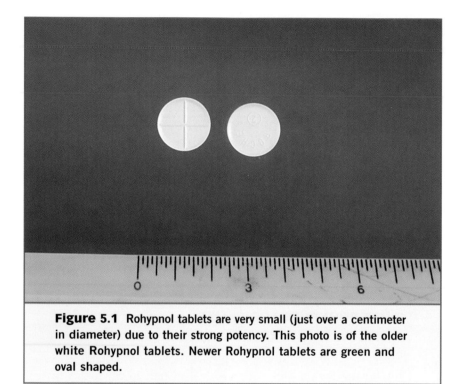

Figure 5.1 Rohypnol tablets are very small (just over a centimeter in diameter) due to their strong potency. This photo is of the older white Rohypnol tablets. Newer Rohypnol tablets are green and oval shaped.

course, he or she is drinking a blue or green drink). Hoffman-La Roche also reduced the dosage of Rohypnol from 1–2 milligrams down to one milligram or less. However, many of the older white pills are still available on the street.

PSYCHOLOGICAL AND PHYSICAL EFFECTS OF ROHYPNOL

Unlike many other designer drugs, which users take for their pleasurable and psychedelic effects, Rohypnol does not tend to produce strong feelings of well-being, euphoria, or hallucinations. It does, however, produce an intoxicated feeling, and reduces anxiety and inhibitions similar to the effects of Valium. The chemical structures of Rohypnol and Valium are very similar (see Figure 5.2), although Rohypnol is ten times more potent than Valium.

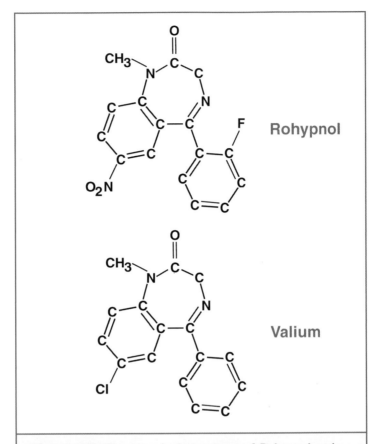

Figure 5.2 The chemical structures of Rohypnol and Valium are shown here. The chemical structure of Rohypnol is quite similar to that of Valium, but Rohypnol is ten times more potent.

The effects of Rohypnol are felt approximately 15–20 minutes after taking the drug and can last up to eight hours. The user will feel drowsy, dizzy, and confused, and may experience extreme sleepiness. Many times the user will become physically and mentally incapacitated, unable to think or move. Despite the strong depressant effects of Rohypnol, some users may initially feel agitated or aggressive. Users often experience "anterograde amnesia," such that he or she will be unable to remember many events that occurred while being under the influence of the drug. Some Rohypnol users take the drug because it lessens the "crash" or depression that follows the high of a stimulant like cocaine or amphetamine.

Physical effects of Rohypnol include gastrointestinal disturbances (an upset stomach), slurred speech, decreased blood pressure, muscle relaxation, motor incoordination, and urinary retention (inability to urinate).

All of the psychological and physical effects of Rohypnol are dramatically increased when the drug is taken in combination with alcohol. In some instances the combination can be lethal.

HOW ROHYPNOL WORKS IN THE BRAIN

Rohypnol, like all benzodiazepines, produces its effect by depressing the activity of nerve cells in the brain. It does so by interacting with a protein called the GABA-A receptor. GABA is the main chemical messenger in the brain that causes nerve cells to become less active. Rohypnol binds to the same protein as GABA (the GABA-A receptor) and increases the ability of GABA to reduce neuronal activity. Other drugs that also act on the GABA-A receptor include alcohol and barbiturates.

Rohypnol is believed to produce its effects by acting on numerous brain regions, as described in Table 5.1.

Table 5.1 Rohypnol's Effect on the Brain

EFFECT	BRAIN REGION(S)
Drowsiness, confusion, dizziness, and sleep	Frontal cortex, brainstem, hypothalamus
Motor impairment	Cerebellum
Slurred speech	Frontal cortex, brainstem
Amnesia	Hippocampus (limbic system)

Rohypnol can also act directly on other parts of the body (i.e., stomach, intestines, bladder, arteries) to produce gastrointestinal disturbances, reduced blood pressure, and urinary retention.

ROHYPNOL—THE ORIGINAL DATE-RAPE DRUG

Although other club drugs (such as GHB and ketamine) can be used to help commit sexual assault, Rohypnol is considered the original "date-rape" drug because it was the first to be used specifically for that purpose. Sexual predators could easily slip the older white tasteless Rohypnol powder into a victim's drink unnoticed, and in less than an hour the victim would become virtually unconscious and mentally paralyzed so the attacker could commit rape without much resistance. Often times the rape victims cannot remember the incident because of the profound amnesia caused by Rohypnol, especially when combined with alcohol. The extensive use of Rohypnol in sexual assaults and "date rapes" in the 1990s prompted Congress to pass the Drug-Induced Rape Prevention and Punishment Act of 1996, which severely increased punishment for use of Rohypnol for the purposes of committing sexual assault. This law also prompted Hoffman-La Roche to add a dye to the pill to allow it to be seen after being dissolved in a drink.

STATISTICS AND PATTERNS OF
ROHYPNOL USE AND ABUSE

Rohypnol is mainly used by teenagers and young adults at dance clubs, parties, and raves. A survey conducted in 2001 showed that 1.1 percent of eighth graders had used Rohypnol at least once, while 1.7 percent of high school seniors had used the drug. But, unlike other designer drugs, the majority of users appear to be Hispanic as opposed to Caucasian. This is not surprising, given that Rohypnol is easily obtained from Mexico. Since Rohypnol can reduce the "crash" that follows the high of drugs like cocaine or heroin, it is also used by cocaine and heroin addicts.

There are two common myths that are believed to increase the usage of Rohypnol among young people: (1) it is a pharmaceutical pill sold in sealed bubble packaging, so it is safe and free of contaminants, and (2) it cannot be detected in urine samples.

ILLEGAL SALE OF ROHYPNOL

Rohypnol is illegal in the United States. So, how does it get in the country? The answer is smugglers. Since the pills are very small, Rohypnol tablets can easily be smuggled through the mail, in luggage or on airplanes. Rohypnol is also easily available from pharmacies in Mexico, and smugglers often hide the drug in cars as they cross the border from Mexico to the United States.

The year 1995 produced the largest number of Rohypnol seizures by the DEA thus far, with over 160,000 illegal pills confiscated. In one instance, over 52,000 Rohypnol pills, concealed in plastic bags located inside a car door, were seized by the Louisiana State Police. Also in 1995, the U.S. Border Patrol seized over 57,000 Rohypnol tablets (along with 53 pounds of marijuana) en route from Mexico to Florida.

Seizures of Rohypnol in the United States have declined over subsequent years, with just under 5,000 pills being seized by the DEA in 2000. In May 2000, DEA agents seized approximately 900 pills of Rohypnol that were hidden in a car crossing the border from Mexico into Texas. A few months later, a Tijuana, Mexico, pharmacy operator was arrested by the DEA for illegally shipping Rohypnol pills from a Mexican pharmacy to nearby San Ysidro—a town minutes north of Tijuana in southern California.

In 2001–2002, however, business began to pick up again, and during this time the DEA seized several overnight delivery packages (e.g., FedEx) originating from Colombia that contained up to 11,000 Rohypnol pills each.

Both of these are false—Rohypnol pills are often crushed by dealers into a powder, and this powder may contain many contaminants incorporated by drug dealers. In addition, advances in medical technology can now detect Rohypnol metabolites in bodily fluids for 2–3 days after taking the drug.

Rohypnol is especially dangerous and potentially lethal when used in combination with other drugs such as alcohol. In 1994, the number of emergency room reports that mentioned Rohypnol was only 13, but this number grew to over 500 by the late 1990s; many of these instances also involved the use of alcohol.

Because Rohypnol is banned in the United States, there is an emerging trend for young people to start abusing two other Rohypnol-like drugs that are still legal in the United States: clonazepam (Klonopin®) and alprazolam (Xanax). Both Klonopin and Xanax are benzodiazepines that are used for the treatment of anxiety and insomnia. Although they are less potent than Rohypnol, they can produce similar effects when mixed with alcohol and also have been reported to enhance the effects of heroin.

ROHYPNOL ADDICTION

Although many benzodiazepine drugs such as Valium or Xanax are successfully used for treating problems like anxiety and insomnia, repeated use of these drugs can produce psychological and physical dependence. Rohypnol is no exception. People who take Rohypnol repeatedly can become addicted and may experience seizures, headaches, anxiety, irritability, delirium and hallucinations, and insomnia when they stop taking the drug. These symptoms may last up to one week after stopping chronic use of Rohypnol. The most common treatment for Rohypnol addiction is medically supervised "tapering off," during which time the user continues to take the drug, but in decreasing doses over a period of many weeks to reduce the severity of withdrawal symptoms.

6

Ketamine

COMMON STREET NAMES

K, Special K, Vitamin K, Lady K, Super K, Kat, Kit Kat, Cat Valium, Bump, Jet, Ket, Ketalar, Ketaject, Psychedelic Heroin, Super acid, Super C, Green, Purple, Kelly's Day, Honey Oil, Blind Squid.

HISTORY AND LEGAL STATUS

Ketamine was first synthesized in the 1960s by the Parke-Davis pharmaceutical company, where scientists were developing analogues of phencyclidine (PCP) for use as general anesthetics for surgery. Like PCP, ketamine proved a potent anesthetic, and Parke-Davis patented it for use in both humans and animals in 1966. Around that same time it was first reported that ketamine had profound psychedelic effects and was named a "dissociative" anesthetic. By the late 1960s, ketamine became available by prescription under the trade name Ketalar®, and was also being used as a field anesthetic by the United States during the Vietnam War. Ketamine's anesthetic properties were also used widely in veterinary clinics, pediatric burn cases, and for some dental surgery.

Throughout the 1970s, 1980s, and 1990s the recreational use of ketamine became popular in many parts of the world, primarily because of its psychedelic effects. Some psychologists even used ketamine as an aid in psychotherapy since it gave people "insightful thinking." In the late 1990s, ketamine became popular with teenagers and young adults at "raves," parties, and dance clubs.

In 1995, the DEA added ketamine to its "emerging drugs"

list, signifying that further restrictions on its use might be needed. Indeed, in 1999 ketamine was classified by the DEA and FDA as a Schedule III controlled substance, making it illegal to possess without a prescription or veterinary license.

WHAT KETAMINE LOOKS LIKE
AND HOW IT IS TAKEN

Ketamine is most commonly sold to pharmacies and veterinary clinics in a clear liquid form (Figure 6.1). Illegal users of ketamine inject the drug intravenously or intramuscularly, mix it into a drink, or dip tobacco or marijuana cigarettes into the liquid prior to smoking them. Ketamine liquid is colorless, odorless, and tasteless. This liquid can be easily converted to a white powder by allowing the liquid to evaporate and then collecting the powder residue. This powder can also be mixed into drinks, snorted, or smoked. A typical dose of ketamine costs $20–$25 on the street.

Ketamine dealers have been known to obtain the drug by breaking into veterinary clinics or pharmacies and stealing their supply of the drug. Dealers also get ketamine by diverting shipments of the drug from pharmacies and veterinary clinics in Mexico.

PSYCHOLOGICAL AND PHYSICAL
EFFECTS OF KETAMINE

The chemical structure of ketamine is similar to that of the potent psychedelic PCP (see Figure 6.2). Not surprisingly, ketamine produces many psychedelic effects that are similar to those produced by PCP. However, ketamine's effects are much shorter in duration—a "trip" on ketamine may last only 30–60 minutes, whereas a trip on PCP may last several hours. The onset of ketamine's actions is quite rapid (i.e., within minutes), especially if snorted or injected intravenously.

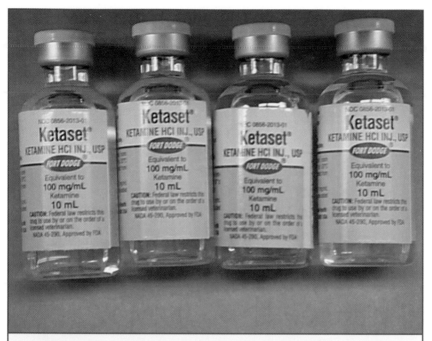

Figure 6.1 Ketamine was originally used in both humans and animals as an anesthetic during surgery. Vials containing the liquid form of ketamine, like the ones pictured here, are still widely used for veterinary purposes.

Lower doses of ketamine (25–100 milligrams) produce an experience that many users call "K-Land," which has been described as a dreamy, relaxed state where the perception of colors and music is enhanced, and mild and pleasurable hallucinations are present. Hallucinations tend to be visual in nature, such as walls and carpets glowing different colors, ceilings turning to liquid, distorted body parts or shapes, and many other illusions. Other hallucinations may include feelings of floating or flying in space, being made out of rubber or wood, spinning and rotating rooms, melting into other people or things, or insight into the meaning of life. Lower doses of ketamine also produce mild amnesia, symptoms of dizziness, and altered perception of sound, taste, and smell.

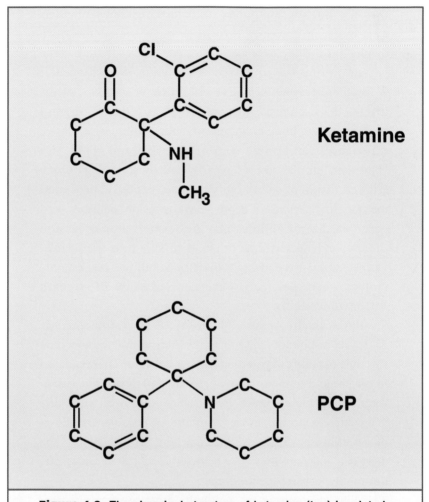

Figure 6.2 The chemical structure of ketamine (top) is related to the psychedelic PCP (bottom). Both chemicals produce strong hallucinations and psychedelic effects. However, while the effects of ketamine may only last an hour, the effects of PCP can last several hours after the drug is taken.

Higher doses of ketamine (more than 100 milligrams) produce more profound psychological effects, sometimes known as the "K-Hole." Here, users often experience "out-of-body" or "near-death" experiences, where they feel like they are floating high above and looking down on their own body, or traveling through a dark tunnel toward a bright light. They may also lose their sense of time—the passage of time may appear to be slowed or even stopped. It is for these reasons ketamine is known as a "dissociative" drug—the user feels "disassociated" and detached from his or her own body and consciousness. These dissociative experiences can also be quite frightening and result in a "bad trip," similar to that experienced by some LSD users. Higher doses of ketamine can also produce profound memory loss, feelings of depression, confusion, delirium, and paranoia. Motor abilities may be severely impaired, and the user may feel as if he or she is unable to move or talk. Occasionally, users of high doses of ketamine can become violent when they feel an exaggerated sense of strength and invulnerability.

Physical effects of high doses of ketamine include decreased respiration and heart rate, increased blood pressure, and the possibility of vomiting and convulsions. These can lead to cardiac and respiratory arrest, coma, and death. The risk of ketamine overdose is much greater when it is mixed with other drugs such as alcohol, Ecstasy, caffeine, or cocaine. Overdoses of ketamine have been reported when people "boost" the drug (i.e., take another dose before the first dose wears off) to prolong its psychedelic effects.

Since ketamine is an anesthetic, most users report profound feelings of numbness. Ketamine users can easily burn themselves on a stove or lamp while on the drug and not even know it.

Ketamine is rapidly metabolized by the body, so the hallucinogenic effects of ketamine wear off within an hour or so after taking the drug. However, users say they often experience repeated "flashbacks," or sudden memories of the visions or feelings experienced while on the drug. These flashbacks can persist for days, weeks, months, or even a year after a particular trip.

HOW KETAMINE WORKS IN THE BRAIN

One of the major neurotransmitters in the brain is an amino acid called glutamate. When neurons secrete glutamate onto a neighboring nerve cell, that neighboring nerve cell becomes activated and passes along the electrical signal to other regions of the brain. Glutamate can activate several types of receptors on nerve cells, and one of the primary subtypes of glutamate receptors is called the N-methyl-D-aspartate (NMDA) receptor. When NMDA receptors are inhibited or "blocked" by certain drugs, nerve cells in the brain that use glutamate as a neuro-transmitter cannot communicate properly.

Ketamine acts as a blocker (or "antagonist") of the NMDA receptor. PCP also acts as an antagonist of the NMDA receptor, as does alcohol, although much less potently. NMDA receptors are present in numerous brain regions, and ketamine is thought to produce its effects by blocking NMDA receptors in a number of brain regions, as shown in Table 6.1.

Table 6.1 Ketamine's Effect on the Brain

EFFECT	BRAIN REGION(S)
Distorted thoughts, vision, and hearing	Frontal cortex, visual cortex
Dizziness	Frontal cortex, brainstem
Difficulty moving, impaired coordination	Motor cortex, basal ganglia, cerebellum
Numbness	Spinal cord, sensory cortex
Amnesia	Hippocampus (limbic system)
Altered breathing, heart rate	Brainstem

KETAMINE AS A DATE-RAPE DRUG

Ketamine has a variety of properties and produces a number of effects that make it an increasingly popular date-rape drug. These properties and effects are as follows:

- It is colorless, odorless, and tasteless, and can easily be slipped into someone's drink without his or her noticing.

- It often causes the user to feel as if they cannot move, making him or her unable to ward off unwanted sexual advances.

- It impairs the user's senses and judgement for up to 24 hours after taking the drug, even though the initial trip wears off within an hour or so.

- It produces amnesia, so the victim may not even recall that a sexual assault has taken place and may not immediately go to the police.

STATISTICS AND PATTERNS OF KETAMINE USE AND ABUSE

As with other designer and club drugs, ketamine is primarily taken by teenagers and young adults ages 18–25. A survey of middle and high school students found that in 2001, approximately 1.3 percent of eighth grade students had tried ketamine in the past year, whereas 2.6 percent of high school seniors had tried the drug. Ketamine users tend to be predominantly male and Caucasian.

Ketamine is often taken with other drugs, such as cocaine, marijuana, alcohol, and Ecstasy, which greatly increases the risk for overdose. Ketamine tends to be taken by people with a history of experimenting with numerous other drugs. Ketamine is also occasionally taken by physicians and veterinarians, who have easy access to the drug and want to experiment with its psychedelic effects.

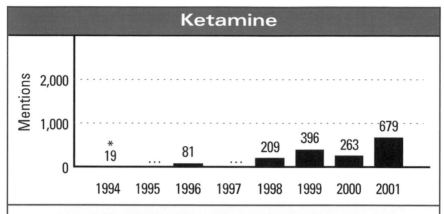

Figure 6.3 Although the number of emergency room mentions of ketamine use is not as high as the rates of methamphetamine and GHB use (see Figures 2.4 and 4.2), ketamine use has increased significantly in the last ten years. The number of emergency room mentions of ketamine nearly doubled between 1999 and 2001.

* The estimate for this year was significantly different (p<0.05) than the estimate for 2001.

Ketamine-related emergency room visits have increased dramatically in recent years (Figure 6.3). In 1994, the number of times ketamine was mentioned in emergency room reports was 19, but by 2001 this number had grown to 679. This increase in ketamine-related emergencies is likely due to its increased popularity at dance clubs and raves, and its combined use with alcohol and other drugs.

While some people use ketamine regularly, others may stop using it because off the K-Hole experience—that near-death/out-of-body experience that is seen with higher doses of the drug. K-Hole experiences increase in frequency with repeated use of ketamine, and these frightening "bad trips" may actually deter people from future ketamine use.

KETAMINE ADDICTION
Although ketamine is used primarily for recreational purposes, cases of addiction to ketamine have been reported. As with

most addictive substances, repeated use of ketamine can produce tolerance, requiring the user to take more and more of the substance to achieve its desired effects. Also, chronic use of ketamine can lead to physical and/or psychological dependence, resulting in withdrawal symptoms once the user stops taking

KETAMINE USE IN TRANQUILIZER DARTS

The ability of ketamine to render the user unable to move or experience pain has resulted in a very effective use for the drug in animals—tranquilizer darts. Through a blowgun, rifle, or similar method, a dart or syringe loaded with a high dose of ketamine can be launched from a distance toward a large animal to incapacitate it for transport, research, or veterinary care. When the dart strikes the animal, it empties its content into the muscle (similar to an intramuscular injection in humans), and within minutes the animal is knocked out. Ketamine darts have been used by zookeepers, wild animal researchers, and veterinarians to tranquilize horses, bears, elephants, monkeys, tigers, lions, leopards, bobcats, mountain lions, large birds, poisonous snakes, and many other animals. Although ketamine causes the animal's muscles to become rigid, it retains its ability to breathe. Also, as in humans, the drug is metabolized very rapidly, and the effects wear off within an hour.

Obviously, we do not know what, if any, psychedelic experiences an animal may have in response to a ketamine dart. (Perhaps they experience K-Land and K-Hole just like humans.) Animals rarely become violent or agitated after being injected with ketamine, so it is unlikely to produce the psychotic symptoms observed in some human users.

the drug. As with other designer and club drugs, specific treatment programs for ketamine addiction have not yet been developed, although they might become needed if current trends of use and abuse continue.

7

Painkiller Analogues

While most people treat headaches and muscle aches by taking aspirin, Tylenol®, Motrin®, or other over-the-counter pain relievers, chronic and severe pain requires more potent painkillers. Some of the most potent pain relieving drugs that have been discovered are "narcotic analgesics," such as morphine, codeine, Vicodin®, OxyContin®, Demerol, Dilaudid®, and others. These drugs are widely used for the treatment of severe pain and are also used as anesthetics for surgical procedures and childbirth. As narcotic analgesics were originally derived from the opium poppy (Figure 7.1), they are often referred to as "opiate" or "opioid" drugs. However, pharmaceutical companies can now synthesize narcotic analgesics in chemical laboratories and are no longer dependent on using raw opium as the primary ingredient.

Most, if not all, opiate drugs are highly addictive, and it is estimated that over 2 million Americans use prescription narcotic analgesics for nonmedical (i.e., recreational) purposes. This percentage tends to be greater among women. The most common addictive opiate drug that is sold on the street is heroin, but patients who use prescription narcotic analgesics for pain, as well as the doctors who prescribe them, can also become addicted. In the late 1970s and early 1980s, two commonly prescribed opiate painkillers, fentanyl and meperidine, fell into the hands of underground drug chemists who tried to synthesize illegal analogues. These fentanyl and meperidine analogues were among the first "designer drugs."

Figure 7.1 The opium poppy, shown here, is the source of such drugs as opium and heroin. Opium poppies are grown in various regions of the world, including the Middle East, Southeast Asia, and Central and South America. To harvest the opium, growers "nick" the poppies with a knife and let the sappy, raw opium drip out. The opium is then scraped off the poppy and processed into illegal opiate drugs like heroin.

FENTANYL AND ITS ANALOGUES

Fentanyl was introduced to the United States in 1968 by the Janssen Pharmaceutical Company and marketed under the trade name Sublimaze. Its primary purpose was for use as an intravenous anesthetic and analgesic. It is 100 times more potent than morphine in reducing pain, and its duration of action is only thirty minutes (compared to morphine which lasts several hours). Over the years, fentanyl has proved an extremely useful drug, and to this date, it is still widely used for surgeries, childbirth, pain associated with cancer and other diseases, and the treatment of trauma-related injuries. Although fentanyl solutions are often given intravenously, pill forms of the drug are also available.

Due to the success of fentanyl, Janssen and other pharmaceutical companies started to produce other legal fentanyl analogues with a wider range of potency and duration of action, including:

- **Alfentanil**—also known as Alfenta®, it is very short-acting (5–15 minutes), 20–30 times more potent than morphine, and used for dental, diagnostic, and other minor surgical procedures.

- **Sufentanil**—also known as Sufenta®, it is extremely potent (2,000–4,000 times more potent than morphine), and is used for heart surgery and childbirth.

- **Carfentanil**—also known as Wildnil®, it is 10,000 times more potent than morphine and is often used by veterinarians and wild animal researchers to immobilize large animals.

- **Lofentanil**—another extremely potent fentanyl derivative that is 6,000 times stronger than morphine and is very long acting (i.e., hours); so it is used only for prolonged surgical procedures and treatment of multiple trauma-related injuries.

In 1979–1980, some illegal fentanyl analogues appeared that were being sold as substitutes for heroin on the street. Suddenly, a series of more than a dozen mysterious deaths occurred in southern California. Upon autopsy, the victims strongly looked as if they had overdosed on heroin; however, no traces of heroin could be found in their bodies. Later, forensic chemists identified a fentanyl analogue (alpha-methyl-fentanyl) that was present in all of the victims. As it turns out, alpha-methyl-fentanyl was being sold on the streets under the name "China White" (Figure 7.2), because it resembled (and contained) pure synthetic heroin that was produced in Southeast Asia.

Later in the 1980s, other fentanyl analogues started to be found in the tissues of heroin users and overdose victims. One such analogue was 3-methyl-fentanyl (see Figure 7.3), which is 6,000 times more potent than morphine. This drug was found in the tissue of sixteen overdose victims in Pennsylvania in 1988. In all, more than 150 deaths have been attributed to overdoses of illegal fentanyl analogues. It is likely that victims overdose because they think they are injecting heroin and are ignorant to the potency of the fentanyl analogues that they are actually taking. Alpha-methyl-fentanyl became classified as a Schedule I controlled substance in 1982, and 3-methyl fentanyl was similarly classified in 1985.

Fentanyl analogues often come as a fine or coarse powder that is either white or yellowish-white (when sold as "China White"), tan (when sold as "Synthetic Heroin"), or light brown (when sold as "Mexican Brown"). Other names for fentanyl or its analogs include "Goodfella" and "Tango and Cash." Drug dealers often cut (dilute) fentanyl analogues with large amounts of powdered sugar so that the actual drug content is very small (as low as 1 percent). When dealers "cook" the fentanyl analogues, the sugar content can become caramelized, giving it a brownish color. The drugs are mostly injected intravenously but can also be snorted or smoked.

Figure 7.2 China White powder, shown here, is a synthetic form of heroin that is very pure. China White that was tainted with illegal fentanyl analogues, which are hundreds of times more potent than heroin, caused numerous overdoses in heroin addicts in the late 1970s and early 1980s.

Users of fentanyl analogues report that these drugs produce a rapid "rush" or euphoria that is similar to that felt with heroin, followed by a sedated, dream-like state. As analgesics, they also produce a profound loss of pain sensation and have common unwanted side effects such as sleepiness and constipation. However, because they are so potent, fentanyl analogues can

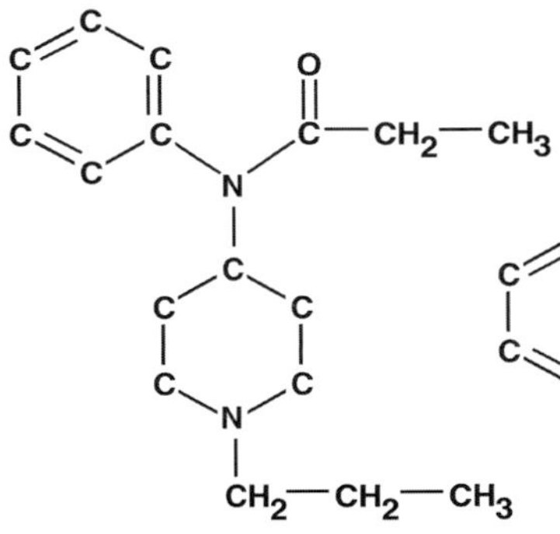

Fentanyl

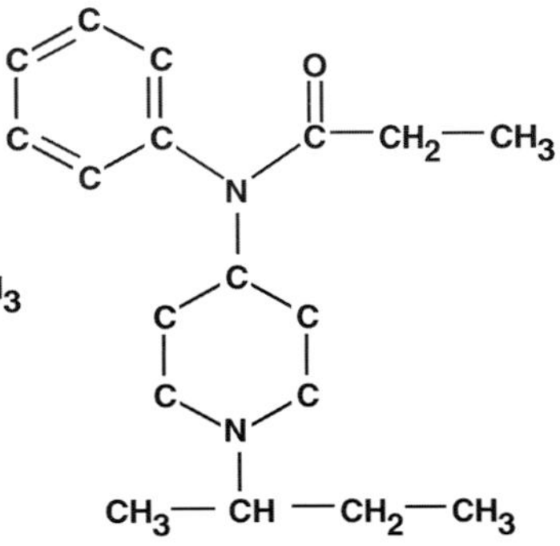

Alpha-Methyl-Fentanyl

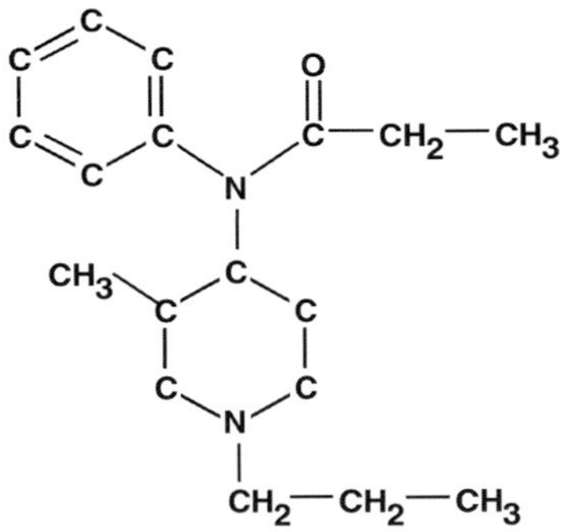

3-Methyl-Fentanyl

Figure 7.3 The chemical structure of fentanyl and its illegal analogues alpha-methyl-fentanyl and 3-methyl-fentanyl are shown here. Fentanyl was originally designed and marketed as an anesthetic, as it is 100 times stronger than morphine. It is still in use today as a pain reliever for certain surgeries, childbirth, and cancer.

easily produce unexpected respiratory paralysis (stopped breathing) and subsequently death. Some law enforcement agents have reported that fentanyl analogue overdose victims often still have the needle in their arm when they are found, likely because the onset of death was so quick.

Opiate painkillers act on a neurotransmitter receptor

called the mu (like the Greek letter m, pronounced "mew") opioid receptor. Mu opioid receptors are present on the surface of many neurons of the brain and spinal cord, and normally serve as receptors for the body's own painkillers such as endorphins. When a person takes fentanyl, meperidine, morphine, or other opiate drugs, the drug binds to the mu opioid receptors, causing neurons in the spinal cord to become inactive. When pain signals from nerve endings in the skin, muscle, or organs arrive at the spinal cord, these signals are not transmitted to the brain, and therefore pain is not experienced. There are also high concentrations of mu opioid receptors in regions of the brainstem that control breathing, so when a person takes an opiate drug, neurons that control breathing become less active and respiration is decreased. Mu opioid receptors are also present in the frontal cortex and limbic system, where opiate drugs act to produce both pleasurable and sedating effects. Finally, mu opioid receptors are present in the intestines, where opiate drugs act to inhibit bowel movements and produce constipation.

MEPERIDINE AND ITS ANALOGUES

Meperidine (Figure 7.4) was introduced in the 1930s as an alternative to morphine for relieving pain. Its advantage over morphine was that its duration of action was shorter and had fewer unwanted side effects such as sedation and constipation.

However, meperidine turned out to be less potent than morphine as a painkiller. This inspired underground chemists to try to synthesize more potent analogues of meperidine, with hopes that increasing the potency might give heroin addicts another way to get high. One such analogue was developed in 1977 by a college student in Bethesda, Maryland, who also had a drug habit. (Ironically, he started making meperidine analogues with a home chemistry kit that his parents gave him.) The analogue he synthesized was 1-methyl-4-phenyl-propionoxypiperidine, or MPPP for short. MPPP was sometimes referred to as a New Heroin.

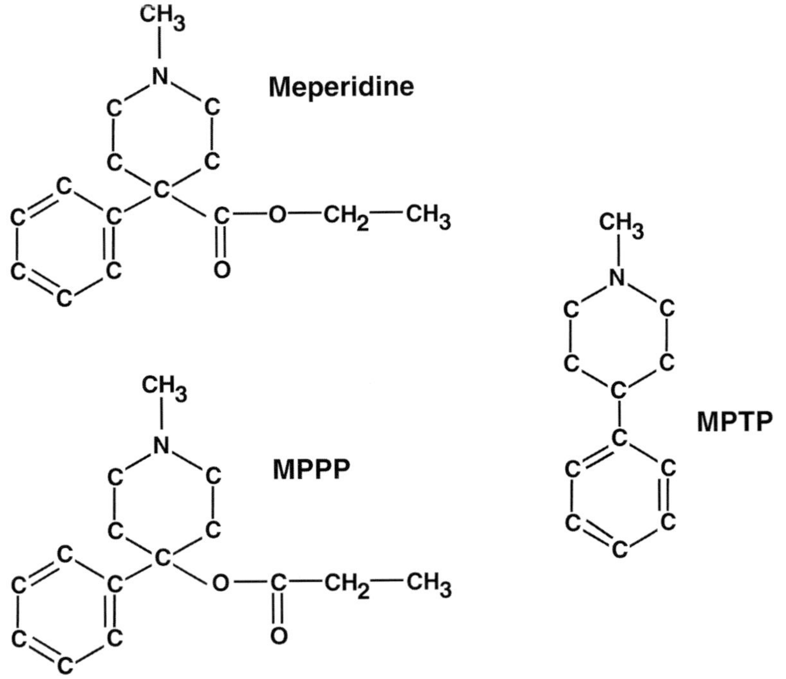

Figure 7.4 The chemical structure of meperidine, its analogue MPPP, and the closely related neurotoxin MPTP, are all shown here. Meperidine, an anesthetic, was also used as an alternative to morphine. It proved advantageous as it has a shorter length of duration and fewer side effects than morphine.

This college student was able to successfully make MPPP from meperidine for months for his own use. However, one day while cooking up some MPPP, he was in a hurry and skipped a step or two in the synthesis process. Later, when he decided to inject himself with this latest batch of MPPP, he immediately knew something was wrong when his whole arm began to burn. Within a few days his arms and legs became completely paralyzed, and he was unable to move or speak. His parents took him to several psychiatrists and neurologists who eventually diagnosed him with Parkinson's disease, a disease that primarily occurs in people over 65 years old and is largely incurable. The college student's life was forever changed.

Unaware of it at the time, the college student's "sloppy chemistry" had, in addition to synthesizing MPPP, inadvertently created some additional by-products that were very toxic. It turns out that one of the by-products, called 1-methyl-4-phenyl-1,2,3,6-tetrahydropyridine (MPTP), is very toxic to neurons in

PARKINSON'S DISEASE— NATURAL AND EXPERIMENTAL

Parkinson's disease is a devastating brain disorder that occurs in approximately one out of every 100 people. The disease is marked by extreme muscle stiffness, slowness or inability to walk, difficulty initiating movements of the arms and legs, and occasionally tremors. Although the disease usually strikes elderly people over the age of 65, it can also occur in younger people. Notable celebrities that have this "early onset" form of Parkinson's disease include boxer Muhammad Ali (who was in his early 40s when diagnosed) and actor Michael J. Fox (who was actually 30 when he was originally diagnosed, but did not go public about the disease for another seven years).

The cause of Parkinson's disease is still unknown. However, researchers have pinpointed the brain regions and neurotrans-mitters involved in the disease. For some reason, neurons containing the neurotransmitter dopamine that are located in a brain region called the substantia nigra (literally, "black substance") start to die in patients with Parkinson's disease. These neurons send their dopamine-releasing axon fibers to the striatum (also known as the caudate nucleus and putamen), a brain region involved in voluntary control of movements. When neurons in the substantia nigra die, a shortage of dopamine in the striatum results, and the patient begins to lose control over muscle movements. Drugs that mimic the

the brain that use the neurotransmitter dopamine. Circuits in the brain that use dopamine are primarily involved in the control of motor skills such as movements of the arms, legs, and face. This MPTP-laced heroin explained why this young man showed signs of Parkinson's disease.

In 1982, many more cases of drug addicts becoming "frozen" after injecting themselves with (what they thought to be) heroin were reported by various emergency rooms in the San Francisco Bay area. Neurologists, psychiatrists, and

action of dopamine, or are converted to dopamine once taken, such as L-dopa, are currently used to treat Parkinson's disease, but with limited success.

When heroin laced with toxic MPTP enters the body, it is metabolized to form MPP+, which is very toxic to neurons containing dopamine, such as those in the substantia nigra. In addition, it is a relatively selective toxin, so it does not destroy neurons containing other types of neurotransmitters. When heroin addicts injected that bad batch of heroin containing the meperidine analogue MPTP, it was converted to MPP+ and destroyed many neurons in their substantia nigra, resulting in a dopamine shortage in their striatum and subsequently symptoms resembling Parkinson's disease.

Despite the misfortunes of these addicts, MPTP has proved an invaluable tool for studying the biology of Parkinson's disease. When MPTP is injected into experimental rats, mice, or monkeys, neurons in the substantia nigra of these animals start to die, and the animals develop motor problems that closely resemble the symptoms of Parkinson's disease. Researchers hope to use MPTP in animals to unravel the mystery of what causes Parkinson's disease in humans, in the hope that they can develop a cure for this devastating disease.

scientists were able to trace contaminants found in the victim's bodies to a bad batch of heroin that was being sold in the area. These unfortunate heroin addicts also developed a form of Parkinson's disease.

Statistics on the patterns of use of fentanyl and meperidine analogues are relatively scarce. While abuse of prescription painkillers is on the rise, the use of fentanyl and meperidine analogues is not. Law enforcement agencies believe the use of painkiller analogues is not nearly as prevalent today as it was in the 1970s and 1980s because of increased law enforcement efforts to shut down illegal underground laboratories and tighter restrictions and documentation of fentanyl and meperidine prescriptions and shipments. In addition, heroin addicts tend to shy away from fentanyl and meperidine analogues because of the frightening reports that they cause frequent overdoses and degeneration of neurons in the brain.

Bibliography and Further Reading

Chapter 1: Designer Drugs and the Brain

Buchanan, J.F., and C.R. Brown. "'Designer drugs.' A problem in clinical toxicology." *Medical Toxicology and Adverse Drug Experience* 3, 1988. 1-17.

Henderson, G.L. "Designer Drugs: Past History and Future Prospects." *Journal of Forensic Science* 33 (1988): 569-575.

Morgan, J.P. "Designer Drugs." In: *Substance Abuse—A Comprehensive Textbook* (Lowinson JH, Ruiz P, Millman RB, Langrod JG, eds). Third Ed. Baltimore: Williams & Wilkins, 1997. 264-269.

Ziporyn, T. "A growing industry and menace: makeshift laboratory's designer drugs." *Journal of the American Medical Association* 256, 1986. 3061-3063.

Chapter 2: Methamphetamine

The DAWN Report. Rockville, Md.: Drug Abuse Warning Network, Office of Applied Studies, Substance Abuse and Mental Health Services Administration (SAMHSA), December 2000.

Emergency Department Trends from the Drug Abuse Warning Network: Final Estimates 1994-2001, Rockville, Md.: Office of Applied Studies, Substance Abuse and Mental Health Services Administration (SAMHSA), August 2002.

Fact Sheet: Methamphetamine. Rockville, Md.: Office of National Drug Control Policy Information Clearinghouse, May 1999.

Monitoring the Future 2002—Data from In-School Surveys on 8th, 10th and 12th Grade Students, Rockville, Md.: National Institute on Drug Abuse and the University of Michigan, December 2002.

Research Report: Methamphetamine Abuse and Addiction, Bethesda, Md.: National Institute on Drug Abuse, NIH Publication 98-4210, April 1998.

Chapter 3: Ecstasy

The DAWN Report. Rockville, Md.: Drug Abuse Warning Network, Office of Applied Studies, Substance Abuse and Mental Health Services Administration (SAMHSA), December 2000.

Emergency Department Trends from the Drug Abuse Warning Network: Final Estimates 1994-2001, Rockville, Md.: Office of Applied Studies, Substance Abuse and Mental Health Services Administration (SAMHSA), August 2002.

Cole, J.C., and H.R. Sumnall. "Altered States: the Clinical Effects of Ecstasy." *Pharmacology and Therapeutics* 98, 2003. 35-58.

Fact Sheet: MDMA (Ecstasy). Rockville, Md.: Office of National Drug Control Policy Information Clearinghouse, May 1999.

Bibliography and Further Reading

Monitoring the Future 2002—Data from In-School Surveys on 8th, 10th and 12th Grade Students, Bethesda, Md.: National Institute on Drug Abuse and the University of Michigan, December 2002.

Chapter 4: GHB

The DAWN Report. Rockville, Md.: Drug Abuse Warning Network, Office of Applied Studies, Substance Abuse and Mental Health Services Administration (SAMHSA), December 2000.

Emergency Department Trends from the Drug Abuse Warning Network: Final Estimates 1994-2001, Rockville, Md.: Office of Applied Studies, Substance Abuse and Mental Health Services Administration (SAMHSA), August 2002.

Fact Sheet: Gamma Hydroxybutyrate. Rockville, Md.: Office of National Drug Control Policy Information Clearinghouse, November 2002.

Monitoring the Future 2002—Data from In-School Surveys on 8th, 10th and 12th Grade Students, Bethedsa, Md.: National Institute on Drug Abuse and the University of Michigan, December 2002.

Chapter 5: Rohypnol

Emergency Department Trends from the Drug Abuse Warning Network: Final Estimates 1994-2001, Rockville, Md.: Office of Applied Studies, Substance Abuse and Mental Health Services Administration (SAMHSA), August 2002.

The DAWN Report. Rockville, Md.: Drug Abuse Warning Network, Office of Applied Studies, Substance Abuse and Mental Health Services Administration (SAMHSA), December 2000.

Fact Sheet: Rohypnol. Rockville, Md.: Office of National Drug Control Policy Information Clearinghouse, February 2003.

Monitoring the Future 2001—Data from In-School Surveys on 8th, 10th and 12th Grade Students, Bethesda, Md.: National Institute on Drug Abuse and the University of Michigan, 2002.

Chapter 6: Ketamine

Curran, H.V. and C. Morgan. "Cognitive, Dissociative and Psychotogenic Effects of Ketamine in Recreational Users on the Night of Drug Use and 3 Days Later." *Addiction* 95, 2000. 575-590.

The DAWN Report. Rockville, Md.: Drug Abuse Warning Network, Office of Applied Studies, Substance Abuse and Mental Health Services Administration (SAMHSA), December 2000.

Emergency Department Trends from the Drug Abuse Warning Network: Final Estimates 1994-2001, Rockville, Md.: Office of Applied Studies, Substance Abuse and Mental Health Services Administration (SAMHSA), August 2002.

Dillon P, Copel and J.K. Jansen. "Patterns of Use and Harms Associated with Non-Medical Ketamine Use." *Drug and Alcohol Dependence* 69, 2003. 23-28.

Monitoring the Future 2002—Data from In-School Surveys on 8th, 10th and 12th Grade Students, Bethesda, Md.: National Institute on Drug Abuse and the University of Michigan, December 2002.

Research Report: Hallucinogens and Dissociative Drugs, Bethesda, Md.: National Institute on Drug Abuse, NIH Publication No. 01-4209, March 2001.

Wenker, C.J. "Anesthesia Of Exotic Animals." *The Internet Journal of Anesthesiology*. Volume 2 Number 3, 1998.

Chapter 7: Painkiller Analogs

Langston, J.W. and J. Palfreman. *The Case of the Frozen Addicts*. New York: Pantheon Books, 1995.

Morgan, J.P. "Designer Drugs." In: *Substance Abuse–A Comprehensive Textbook*. 3rd edition (J.H. Lowinson, P. Ruiz, R.B. Millman, and J.G. Langrod, eds), Baltimore, Md.: Williams & Wilkins, 1997, pp. 264-269.

Research Report: Prescription Drugs: Abuse and Addiction, Bethesda, Md.: National Institute on Drug Abuse, NIH Publication No. 01-4881, July 2001.

Websites

www.health.org

U.S. Department of Health and Human Services and the Substance Abuse and Mental Health Services Administration (SAMHSA)'s National Clearinghouse for Alcohol and Drug Information. Provides information about prevention, treatment, and recovery.

www.whitehousedrugpolicy.gov

The U.S. government's Office of National Drug Control Policy. Legal issues and fact sheets.

www.drugabuse.gov

The National Institute on Drug Abuse's Website. An extensive website containing information for children and parents, teachers and students, and researchers and health professionals.

www.dea.gov

Website of the U.S. Drug Enforcement Administration. Contains legal information about drug use and abuse.

www.clubdrugs.org

A Website targeted toward teenagers, part of the National Institute on Drug Abuse. Focuses on club drugs such as Ecstasy, GHB, Rohypnol, ketamine, methamphetamine, and LSD.

www.streetdrugs.org

Extensive Website devoted to education about many drugs, current trends, and law enforcement policies.

www.methamphetamineaddiction.com

Contains information about methamphetamine addiction, treatment options, and personal stories of recovery. Sponsored by the Narconon Arrowhead treatment program.

www.ecstasyaddiction.com

Information about Ecstasy (MDMA) addiction, treatment options, and personal stories of recovery. Sponsored by the Narconon Arrowhead treatment program.

www.projectghb.org

Information about GHB, the effects of the chemical, and date rape, as well as personal accounts.

www.designer-drugs.com

Personal Website of Donald A. Cooper, Drug Enforcement Administration, McLean, Virginia. Contains information about various synthetic, or "designer" drugs.

Additional Resources

If you would like more information about drug use and abuse, or to speak to someone confidentially, please call the following hotlines:

American Council for Drug Education
  800-488-DRUG (800-488-3784)

National Institute of Drug Abuse
  888-644-6432

National Council on Alcoholism and Drug Dependence, Inc's Hope Line
  800/NCA-CALL

National Treatment and Referral Hotline1
  1-800-662-HELP

Or visit the **Substance Abuse and Mental Health Services Administration** (SAMHSA)'s treatment facility locator Website at *http://findtreatment.samhsa.gov/facilitylocatordoc.htm* to find a treatment facility near you.

For Parents and Teachers:
If you would like information about how to talk to your children or students about drugs and alcohol, or to learn more about drug abuse in teens, please visit the following Websites:

A Family Guide to Keeping Youth Mentally Healthy and Drug Free, provided by the Substance Abuse and Mental Health Services Administration (SAMHSA) *http://family.samhsa.gov/*

Partnership for a Drug Free America
  www.drugfreeamerica.org

Parents. The Anti-Drug
  www.theantidrug.com

Drug Strategies: Treating Teens
  Web companion to the Drug Studies publication: *Treating Teens: A Guide to Adolescent Drug Programs* *http://www.drugstrategies.org/teens/index.html*

Talk With Your Kids
Information on talking with your children about various tough issues,
including drug abuse.
http://www.talkingwithkids.org/

Drugstory.org. Information about Drug Prevention and Treatment,
sponsored by the Office of National Drug Control Policy
http://www.drugstory.org/prevention_treatment/index.asp

Index

Index

Picture Credits

Alfenta is a registered trademark of Johnson & Johnson; Demerol is a registered trademark of Sanofi-Synthelabo Inc.; Desoxyn is a registered trademark of Abbott Laboratories; Dilaudid is a registered trademark of Knoll Pharmaceutical; Ketalar is a registered trademark of Warner Lambert Company; Klonopin is a registered trademark of Hoffman LaRoche Inc.; M&M is a registered trademark of Mars Inc.; Motrin is a registered trademark of Johnson & Johnson; Mountain Dew is a registered trademark of PepsiCo. Inc.; OxyContin is a registered trademark of Purdue Pharma Inc.; Pez is a registered trademark of Pez Candy Inc.; Prozac is a registered trademark of Eli Lilly and Company; Ritalin is a registered trademark of Novartis; Rohypnol is a registered trademark of Hoffman LaRoche Inc.; Skittles is a registered trademark of Mars Inc.; Sublimaze is a registered trademark of Johnson & Johnson; Sudafed is a registered trademark of Warner Lambert Company; Sufenta is a registered trademark of Johnson & Johnson; Tylenol is a registered trademark of McNeil Consumer Brands; Valium is a registered trademark of Hoffman LaRoche Inc.; Viagra is a registered trademark of Pfizer Inc.; Vicodin is a registered trademark of Knoll Pharmaceuticals Company; Wildnil is a registered trademark of Johnson & Johnson; Xanax is a registered trademark of Pharmacia & Upjohn Company; Xyrem is a registered trademark of Orphan Medical Inc.

About the Author

M. Foster Olive received his Bachelor's in Psychology from the University of California at San Diego, and went on to receive his Ph.D. in neuroscience from UCLA. He is currently an associate investigator at the Ernest Gallo Clinic & Research Center, a non-profit research institute affiliated with the Department of Neurology at the University of California at San Francisco. His research focuses on the neurobiology of stress and addiction, and is published in numerous academic journals including *Pharmacology, Biochemistry and Behavior, Psychopharmacology*, and the *Journal of Neuroscience*. Foster and his family live in the San Francisco Bay Area in northern California.

About the Editor

David J. Triggle is a University Professor and a Distinguished Professor in the School of Pharmacy and Pharmaceutical Sciences at the State University of New York at Buffalo. He studied in the United Kingdom and earned his B.Sc. degree in chemistry from the University of Southampton and a Ph.D. degree in chemistry at the University of Hull. Following post-doctoral work at the University of Ottawa in Canada and the University of London in the United Kingdom, he assumed a position at the School of Pharmacy at Buffalo. He served as Chairman of the Department of Biochemical Pharmacology from 1971 to 1985 and as Dean of the School of Pharmacy from 1985 to 1995. From 1995 to 2001 he served as the Dean of the Graduate School and as the University Provost from 2000 to 2001. He is the author of several books dealing with the chemical pharmacology of the autonomic nervous system and drug-receptor interactions, some 400 scientific publications, and has delivered over 1,000 lectures worldwide on his research.